James Masters

FOOD PARCELS TO READING

Published by CreateSpace 2013

All Rights Reserved

No part of this publication may be reproduced, stored in any other retrieval system, or transmitted in any form, without the prior written permission of the author, nor be otherwise circulated in any form or binding or cover other than that in which it is published and without a similar condition being imposed on the subsequent publisher.

Cover design is by the Author.

Foreword

I really didn't expect the enormous success of my first book "Fated . . ." but due to that and also the fantastic comments and encouragement to write another book by its readers; "Food Parcels to Reading" evolved.

"FP2R" tells the story of a young ruffian who was brought up in the harsh streets of downtown Middlesbrough, but was transformed by his mother and the strict grammar school that he went to.

Initially he rebelled against all authority figures involved in this process – often with hilarious results, but after failing his exams, he decided to stick in and very unexpectedly, qualified through Reading University to become a PE teacher.

Whilst in teaching, many of his ex-pupils probably noticed some of the rough edges that still remained, but after reading this book they will probably understand why.

It also explains why he related so well, and understood the problems encountered by, some of the less privileged kids in his schools.

It is written in the same easy to read and humorous style of the first book, with probably just as many grammatical, spelling and structural errors, so I hope that readers enjoy FP2R as much as "Fated . . ." and can overlook the mistakes of a ham fisted ex-PE teacher.

*   *   *

This is what Simon said:- *(not a game !!!)*
"I think this book is better than the first, but that's not saying I didn't like the first. They are both enjoyable reads, but this one just edges out the first!

I caught myself laughing out loud on quite a few occasions.

I think people will relate to a lot of things in the book, probably more people will say 'yeah, that was me' even though it wasn't!

It will remind them of what little t***s they were at school! and how hard it is/was being their teacher."

Enjoy,
James

Food Parcels to Reading

This book is dedicated to the teachers of Acklam Hall Grammar School in Middlesbrough; who changed my life.

In particular, Georgia Naylor, who was my greatest mentor & influence and, most importantly, who believed in me.

Also, Ken Midgeley and Peter Illingworth who were willing to give me a chance.

But, finally, the rest of the staff who taught me how *not* to deal with kids.

I succeeded despite them.

Contents

Page 1   Credits

Page 2   Foreword

Page 3   Dedication

Page 5   Contents

Page 6   Chapter 1 - Mam to the Rescue

Page 31   Chapter 2 - A Culture Shock

Page 64   Chapter 3 - A Different Boy

Page 93   Chapter 4 - Hitch – Hiking plus

Page 127 Ch. 5 - Food Parcels to Reading

Page 153 Ch. 6 - Top That

Page 179 Ch. 7 - Life Off Campus

Page 211 Ch. 8 - My Final Year

Page 241 Ch. 9 - Holiday Jobs

Page 271 Other Publications by the Author

Chapter 1
Mam to the rescue

I was born at a very young age into the harsh streets of one of the poorest areas of Middlesbrough: - Newport.

I was constantly warned by 'me Mam' about playing over Cannon Street, which was the roughest part of the district, but, unfortunately this just made it even more of a magnet to me. Besides, most of my friends from junior school lived over there; but the real pull was that the streets were like an adventure playground.

The Second World War had ended just five years before I was born, and much of Cannon Street was still rubble from the constant bombing it received, courtesy of the Luftwaffe.

Just beyond Cannon Street was the Newport Bridge over the River Tees, and the Railway Station. The shipping, carrying steel from Dorman Long and chemicals from ICI, and the trains/tracks were the real targets of the errant German bombers, but unfortunately Newport bore more than its fair share of stray bombs.

It was reported in the Evening Gazette, that in just one raid in August 1942, 1156 people were made homeless whilst 28 people were killed by the German airforce.

Most of this rubble had been taken away by lorries, but there was still sufficient left for it to be a hoard of hidden treasure for us youngsters. My best mate, Derek, found a bayonet there once. Of course, his Dad took it off him, but for an hour or so he was the hero of our 'gang' showing us all how he would use it if one of those bloody 'Nazzi's' dared set foot in our street.

(note: Nazi is spelt how Derek pronounced it!!!)

I found a old metal war helmet that stank of ashes and soil, but nevertheless, proudly wore it as a crash helmet everytime (which was often) that we had a 'bogie' race down the back alleys of Laws Street and Bennett Street.

*   *   *

"You've been over Cannon Street again, haven't you?" Mam would yell when I came in, once again pitted with dirt and grime from my adventures.

"No Mam, I've only been as far as Bennett Street."

"Don't lie to me," she would shout back, "How many times have I told you not to go there. AND to stay away from those Thorpe twins."

"But Mam, Derek Thorpe is me best mate from school."

"Well, stay away from him. He's always in trouble, and he'll get you into trouble too!"

Mam was right. Derek and his twin brother, were always in trouble and probably, if fate hadn't lent a hand, and I hadn't passed the 'Eleven Plus' and gone to grammar school, I'd have ended up in Durham Jail just like they did.

Initially, Mam and me lived with Gran in a three up three down rented house at 363 Newport Road. Dad had spent most of the war as a prisoner in Lower Selesia (now Poland) and afterwards much of the time recuperating, and later working, with the Army at Aldershot.

That great thing called progress means that 363 is no longer there 'cos they knocked it down when they built Cannon Park and the roundabout off the A66 dual carriageway.

This was just as well really, 'cos although I loved that house, nowadays it would have been called a slum. It had no indoor toilet and no bathroom.

Sunday night was always 'bath night' when the old tin bath was dragged out of the backyard by my Uncle Kenny. He hosed it around to get rid of any spiders or cobwebs and then placed it in front of the roaring fire in the living room. Then the girls (Mam and me aunties) went through the ritual of putting loads of kettles and pans on the gas stove to heat up, and then they set about erecting a screen around the bath. This screen comprised of everybody's own almost threadbare towel, which had been washed, ironed & aired, from the previous week, which was hung across a clothes horse in the order that they could bathe in relative privacy. A strict pecking order was closely adhered to:- oldest first down to the youngest.

So, Gran got in first and had the advantage of the cleanest, but shallowest, water - and the youngest, who went last, obviously had deeper but well used water.

This should have been me, but fortunately I was still so small that I could take my bath in the huge, rectangular, stone kitchen sink - which of course was filled up with warm, *clean* water.

As mentioned, the other great hardship of the house, was that the toilet was outdoors!

No problem, and very hygienic, during those warm, balmy summer nights which we seemed to get loads of in those days - *But* the winters were harsh!!!

As I grew older it became my job to make sure that the toilet paper never ran out, so I had to tear up squares of the Sunday paper (normally 'The People') put a hole in the top corner, and thread the string through, on which it hung on the back of the draughty, wooden door. Even in those days I was very creative, and considered writing to the newspaper with my advertising slogan "The Sunday People – The Best Paper To Wipe Your A**e On!"

As I became even older I acquired an even more vital job – to ensure that the paraffin heater never ran out of fuel, and that it was lit before nightfall when winter cold set in. If I failed in my duties on either of these jobs I got a clip around the ear from whoever was the unfortunate to then go into the freezing loo.

Our family were considered the posh ones in this area 'cos we could afford a paraffin heater *and* Sunday papers.

The heater was both a luxury and a necessity, because, of course, the toilet in the winter was genuinely *freezing* cold. So, to sit there at minus two would have been torture, but it was also a necessity because without it the water in the cistern, pipes, and toilet bowl would very quickly ice over. *(with very smelly consequences.)*

As I grew older, sometime after 6 years old, Dad returned from the Army, and took various jobs as a driver, but the best one as far as the family was concerned was the one he kept the longest; working for Erimus Cleaners on Linthorpe Road. This was not only the best paid of his jobs, but also as he took on the role of caretaker, and Mum also worked as a supervisor with the same company, we were offered accommodation above the premises.

The flat was luxurious compared to our previous lodgings, as I now had my own bedroom, and we also had a 'proper' bathroom, with *indoor toilet*. We even had proper toilet paper, even though it was the awful rough and shiny, non-absorbent Izal - it was still a step up from 'The People'.

The only problem with the premises on Linthorpe Road was that Erimus was a *Dry Cleaners* and the smell of the chemicals that they used in the process constantly drifted upstairs to our flat. Everything, including our lungs and clothes, was permeated by it. So Mum couldn't wait to move out.

She scrimped and saved to get together a deposit in order to acquire a mortgage on our own house in the 'poshest' part of Newport – Laycock Street.

If it had been down to Dad we would never have made this move, because he would have spent every penny on boozing and gambling.

Before the war Dad was practically a professional gambler. He would work mornings as a caddy at one of his local golf courses in Surrey, and in the afternoon would generally treble these earnings, at one of the numerous racetracks. He was very good, even though he never had much of a permanent job anywhere – always unskilled or semi-skilled work – his brain was like a computer when it came to the horses. He knew every horse, every jockey, every trainer – how the horse fared last time out, over what distance, how much weight it carried, etc. He was amazing.

If only he had applied this intelligence to a career. But unfortunately no, and our life when he gambled was very up and down. Like all gamblers he never thought the bubble would burst. When he was winning he didn't put any money away 'for a rainy day' but bought drinks for everybody and treated all of his friends to a free day out at the next race meeting. Of course when he went on a losing streak – as all gamblers do – his huge group of friends all suddenly disappeared. *(surprise!)*

When he was on one of his downers this always caused huge arguments in the family, because he would always come home begging for money for his next stake from Mum.

"Come on, Nance," he would plead, "this one's a certainty.

"All of your horses are certainties" she would reply.

"Aw, come on, Nance, I'll give you it straight back after the race."

"You are not risking the kid's money."She would snap back, "This is for next week's school dinners, and he needs some school shoes. There's a hole in the one's he's wearing now."

Then the yelling would begin, he would throw pots, I've even seen his dinner, that Mum slaved over, thrown up the kitchen wall – BUT to his credit he never laid a finger on Mum, me, or any of the (future) kids.

It was witnessing scenes like this that persuaded me never to get into gambling. Alright, I put a few quid on the Grand National once a year, and I occasionally do the National Lottery, but I can walk away from it all.

Dad couldn't.

It was like a disease to him. I became sick of the number of times he told me what he was going to buy me when *(not if)* his Littlewoods Pools coupon came up.

All I can say (now that he's deceased) – is, what a waste of a good brain – but also thank God for Mum who held our family together. If it hadn't been for her we wouldn't have had any holidays, I wouldn't have gone to grammar school, and we would have been walking around in raggy clothes with empty bellies.

Also, as already stated, Mum was directly responsible for us owning our own house in the poshest street in the area. All my friends at school were really jealous, most of them lived in rented houses in very cramped conditions. The Thorpe twins, for example, lived in a two bedroomed house with five others. Mum and Dad shared the main bedroom, The 9 year old twins and Gran had the second bedroom, whilst 7 year old Wendy slept on the settee in the Living

Room with 4 year old Bobby curled up on a pile of overcoats in the corner. The wall paper, in most rooms was tattered and hanging off. They regularly only ate a packet of crisps for dinner, but on a day when their mum had some money, they would share 2 bags of chips, (with scraps) from the local Fish Shop, between four of them.

Holidays for them were unheard of – in fact I don't think they had even travelled the ten miles to the nearest seaside resort of Redcar.

So, imagine how they felt when 'the posh kid' went away for a week to Whitby, Staithes, or Robin Hood's Bay.

Fortunately, once again, Mum was right when she insisted, against my protestations, that I went to the local grammar school;

"But, Mam, all me friends are going to Stainsby. *(cue Chis Rea – who got on the same school bus as me,)* I won't know anyone at Acklam Hall."

"I'm not arguing, Acklam Hall is the best school. You've passed the 'Eleven Plus', you've been given a chance to better yourself - you're not wasting it!"

"OK, Brackenhoe then, that's a good school and you get a good job when you leave there."

"ACKLAM HALL!"

"But, Mam, it's full of snobs. - - - Middlesbough High School, then!"

"One more word from you, and you go straight to bed without any Tea!

So, Acklam Hall it was, and it saved my life.

If I'd have gone to one of the other schools that I insisted on, I would have 'cruised' through lessons instead of being pushed. OK, I was bright enough to have passed the exams, and would probably have gone on to getting an apprenticeship and learned a trade *(probably ending up being very rich, running my own business)*. But, just as easily, judging by my current circle of friends, I might have been drawn into a life of crime.

I think I was too smart to be banged up in prison for petty crime like the Thorpe's, but who knows what would have happened? I had already started my 'apprenticeship' with them.

Derek & me got up to the usual juvenile petty shoplifting, that was commonplace for the kids from our area.

Nothing much, just a couple of potatoes from Pybus' the grocers, to put in the bonfire in November and a couple of plastic soldiers from 'Woolies,' but the hairiest venture was nicking lead from the gasworks. Not because it was harder to steal, but it was the fact that we had to outrun the watchman's Alsatian dog, once he'd spotted us. Fortunately for me, I was like a whippet, but also more intelligent than the other 'gang members'. After we climbed the broken glass topped wall, I looked for the nearest pipes to remove the lead from and also planned my escape route for when I heard the dog barking. Poor Paul Grabham wasn't so astute, when he heard the dog bark and the watchman yelling, he panicked. He ran the wrong way, *into* the compound and in total pandemonium stated to climb up the gasometer's steps - one way up, and only one way down. Paul made it to the first level, but with the man and dog closing in behind him – he realised his mistake and jumped.

He broke his leg in three places.

The police and an ambulance were called.

Being Saturday and with Paul being in hospital, we didn't know exactly what had happened until we returned to school on Monday.

We weren't stupid enough to go around to his house to enquire, because that would, of course, implicate us. Also in those days there were no mobile phones, and only the rich could afford to have a phone in their house. There were also no computers, no email, no twitter or facebook. So we were left completely in the dark.

I was crapping myself.

For a day and a half I didn't sleep. Everytime there was a knock on the door I ran upstairs, thinking it was the police,

This incident, more than the others that follow, convinced me that it was too risky to follow an illegal lifestyle. I was too young then to realise that although I was surrounded by the criminal fraternity in Newport, I would meet just as many crooks later in life that worked in politics, the City, business, etc. (They were just better dressed, better educated and better spoken) – Give me the 'honest' people of Newport anytime!

Monday morning – eventually – came around.

Me and the Thorpe twins were relieved that poor Peter hadn't grassed us up, when Mr. Dodgson, our form teacher, told us, whilst looking sternly at me, and the Thorpes, that "the police are still looking for three children that ran away from the scene."

"If anybody knows anything about this, you can tell me about it and I will inform the police."

I looked across at Derek and Phil – butter wouldn't have melted in their mouths, and as Dodgson looked at me for any tell tale signs, I simply stared straight back again, with my most angelic, wide eyed, expression.

We unanimously agreed to leave it a few weeks before going to the local 'dodgy' scrap merchant with the lead. We also, as a sensible precaution, melted the lead down into fishing weights and told the dealer that our big brother had sold his fishing rod, and so had no use for the weights. He, no doubt, knew exactly where the lead had come from but accepted our story, and the false names and addresses that we gave.

As for Paul Grabham, he was hauled over the coals by the police when they interviewed him, but as we were all only ten years old at the time, he was let off with a warning of what would happen to him, when he was older, if he continued in this vein.

This run in with the police had its effect - nearly six months had passed before I suffered my next similar sleepless night.

It was close to Bonfire Night, and, as was commonplace in our area, we had all managed to buy some fireworks weeks in advance. It was bitter cold so most of us had the hoods up on our very fashionable duffel coats as we fooled around throwing bangers at each other. Then Phil suggested that we had a war game. His team would defend their fort – which was an old, open back, lorry that had stood, abandoned, for months, on Silkburn Common. The other 'army' would attack them and try to capture it. So we picked up teams and mine, which consisted of Derek, Jeremy Hawke (Jez) and myself, had to count to a hundred before the 'war' started. We hid in a back alley and discussed tactics.

We counted to roughly a hundred before we shouted "Coming"

Me and Thorpy attacked the front of the fort, creating a diversion by throwing as many bangers as quickly as possible whilst Jez had to sneak round the back, as secretly as possible, and climb up the side of the lorry to take their army prisoner.

All went according to plan, as all three of their army concentrated on me and

Thorpy, and were repelling the attack on our side of the lorry. It would have worked too, and we should have won the battle, - if Jez had stuck to the plan. But, just as he got to the back of the lorry, I glanced over to see how close we were to capturing them, when I saw him falter. He then attempted to put a firework into the petrol tank.

I ran towards him shouting "Don't, if there's any petrol . . ." - just as the explosion lifted me off my feet.

I was blown, I guessed, about ten yards and was face down on the rough, black, coal dust covered earth. As I recovered, I arched my back and looked at the floor. The blackness was now a very hazy and orange colour. I decided that my eyesight had been damaged and was squinting and testing it when I heard the man's voice.

"Hey, you little buggers. What have you done? Come here. I'm getting the police."

Instinctively, I got to my feet and ran. I stumbled badly as my vision was very blurred. My eyesight was, fortunately, rapidly recovering, but my face was feeling very sore due to my eyebrows and fringe being burnt off. Luckily the hood of my duffel coat protected the rest of my head.

But, there was no time to fret over my injuries, 'The Man' was gaining on me as I stumbled. Then the adrenalin kicked in, and I was a whippet again. I soon built up a gap of twenty metres on our chaser and as I pulled further away he decided to end the pursuit. I ran round a corner and there was a wide eyed Derek Thorpe just ahead of me. I caught up with him, and he blurted "Have we lost him?"

I nodded and then he started laughing.

I kept running, thinking he was mad and delirious, but still wanting to put some more distance between myself and the explosion.

Thorpy ran with me intermittently chuckling and crying. Then as we turned into a back alley I saw what he was laughing at. Jez Hawke was ahead of us, yelling and screaming, and jumping up and down as he tried to put out the flames from his hair with both hands.

He was obviously in big trouble, and it wasn't funny – but I couldn't help it. It all looked so funny. I joined Thorpy in the laughter.

We followed Jez to his house, but when he opened the door, we scarpered; too scared to see what Mr or Mrs Hawke had to say.

When I got home my Dad exclaimed "Your in early, what's up?"

"Nowt" I yelled back, as I galloped up the stairs to the bathroom.

In the bathroom, no amount of Brylcreem and combing would bring back the lost hair or eyebrows.

I heard Dad's footsteps on the stairs.

Game up; - I blurted out the story.

Dad was quite calm about it, but Mum was furious.

Next day she sent a note into school, explaining why I had no eyebrows and flaky skin. Mr. Dodgson read it out to the class as a warning. As I stood out the front, most of them just stared at me and giggled. Of course the Thorpe twins didn't bother turning up that day to share my embarrassment – but my Mum insisted that I owned up, - and part of my punishment was to face the class and the teachers.

I still didn't know until that night what had happened to the other 'team' in the lorry, but there they were at our gang meeting place without a scratch. Apparently when the petrol tank exploded they were all blown out of the back like human cannonballs. They saw The Man chasing us, so all scarpered in the opposite direction.

Very luckily, all of our injuries were minor, except for Jez. He was kept in hospital for about 3 months. He had to have numerous skin grafts, his hearing was damaged, and he had to have his right ear rebuilt as it was totally burnt off by the fire.

We were all thankful that it wasn't us, but in hindsight *it was* Jez who was daft enough to put a firework into a petrol tank, so poetically, justice really!

Now that School and the Hospital knew about our escapade, I spent about a week of sleepless nights, waiting for the Police to call.

Personally, I wasn't as afraid of the police as I was of my mother. Different to most families in our area at the time, my father never laid a finger on me, or my two brothers, but it was Mam who was the disciplinairian.

In one particular incident I had taken Derek Thorpe home for tea (it must have been before he was finally banned), and we were reading one of our favourite 'Commando' comic books.

"No wonder the Germans flattened Cannon Street with their bombs," I told

Thorpy, "some of them could carry more than ten tons!"

"Ten tons, is that heavy?" Derek asked

"Ten tons! Is that f*****g heavy?" I blurted out, "That's . . ."

I didn't get the rest of the sentence out, when W-H-A-C-K, my head felt like it had left my shoulders and bounced off the chimney breast.

"What did you say then??? WHAT did you say?" Mam screamed.

I hadn't realised that she could hear us from the kitchen, where she was baking some scones.

"Where did you learn language like that?"

Fighting back the tears, I confessed, "Cannon Street, Mam."

"Cannon Street???" She switched her glare to Derek.

"How many times have I told you to stay away from there?"

I didn't answer, but just looked at Derek for support – it didn't come. Thorpy was stunned; firstly because he had never seen me Mam react like that before, but mainly because he didn't see anything wrong - swearing like that was commonplace in his house.

It, however, was never heard again in my house, neither from me nor from either of my parents.

Derek Thorpe never came into my house again.

*   *   *

As mentioned, going to grammar school saved me from all of this – but it wasn't easy.

It started with the name calling. After I had been accepted to Acklam, suddenly overnight I had become a snob, and couldn't join in many of the gang's adventures 'cos I would get me hands dirty, but the culmination was when my proud mother took me to get my new School uniform from the most expensive 'rip off' school retailers in the town.

I had to be fitted with my new blazer – black with green & white piping around the lapels; neatly pressed grey, short trousers, and grey, knee length socks with a black, green & white turnover. I looked like Little Lord Fauntleroy – I hated it – but what I hated most of all was the little leather satchel that I had to wear on my back to carry my books.

"But, I don't need that Mam, I'll carry my books in me hand."

"There might be too many of them"

"I'll take them in a carrier bag then!"

I don't know if she even heard me, or just ignored me, "and then there's your PE kit, you can't carry all of that in your hand."

"Well, I'll have a haversack then like David Jay and Johnny Hull"

(David & Johnny were two lads from the 'Street' who had gone to Acklam in previous years)

I should have known it was useless arguing.

So on my first day at Acklam Hall Grammar School (for young gentlemen) I stood, like a tailor's dummy, in our living room – with my satchel on my back – having my photograph taken by my proud Mam and my Aunties. Then, with tears rolling down Mam's face, she kissed me (Mam never normally kissed me!) and pushed me out the front door before I had a chance to struggle.

Out on the now unusually enormous Street, I glanced to my right and then my left to make sure nobody had spotted me, and then I became a whippet again. I didn't stop running until I got to school two miles away.

Mum had given me bus fare, but I couldn't bear the thought of all those people looking at me in my uniform, so I ran.

Later I learnt, that running to School saved enough bus fare money to buy an 'ice cream oyster' from the van that stopped outside the School gates every dinnertime, so my first taste of athletics training had just begun.

As I rounded the corner of Hall Drive, I fumbled for my cap in my pocket and I put it on, 'cos David & Johnny had already warned me that it was an automatic detention if any boy was caught out of school, in uniform, without wearing a cap.

And, you couldn't spot the prefects who were waiting outside of the School checking especially for this offence.

I found this difficult to accept – but 'prefects'? – what's that all about?

I, also, found it difficult to understand the School rule that boys must wear short trousers until they reached the fifth form!!! It was comical to see some of the six foot three, fourth form boys walking in to school, with their big hairy legs protruding from their short trousers, and with a tiny black and green quartered cap precariously perched on top of a huge shock of unruly hair.

The first day was a nightmare. It seemed to mainly consist of being told of what we couldn't do, and places we couldn't go - and the equipment we would need.
Oh, and we also were given our timetable.

Timetable? what's that for??? We never had one of *those* at Newport School, and what's with all this French and Algebra, and Geometry. And what's a pair of compasses?

We EVEN got a timetable for . . .
Homework

Homework !!! Stuff that! As soon as I get home I'm going out to play footie on Laycock Rec. with the 'gang'. I'll 'ave a look at the 'omework when it gets dark!

When the bell rang for the end of the day my brain was hurting. I'd never done so much thinkin' before, I couldn't wait to get home and get me old clothes on and me football out.

So, after the two mile *walk* home, as I turned the corner from Carlow Street and walked past the 'Rec', a huge smile crossed my face, I was really looking forward to enjoying a great game of soccer.

The smile was soon wiped off my face, however, as I heard the rustle of the bushes.

"Right lads, get him!" The Thorpes and two more of the gang jumped me and dragged me on my back through a huge muddy puddle in front of the bush that they had hidden behind. They then repeated the procedure for the front of my uniform, before running off shouting "There yer are ye snob – don't look so flash now, do yer?"

I suppose that was their way of telling me that I was out of the gang.

It worked.

Chapter 2

A Culture Shock

I think it was the behavioural psychologist, Eysenk, who said that a person's personality was 30% inborn (genetic) and 70% affected by environment.

In that case, I was perfect proof of his theory because my new environment certainly changed my whole outlook on life *and my personality*– BUT it was painful!

For the first two years at Acklam Hall I rebelled against everything that the School was trying to turn me into. I think I was probably the most slippered boy in the first year; I certainly held the record for detentions. My 'proud' Mum was only too pleased that I began coming home late on a very regular basis due to my excuses of attending rugby or basketball training and even the Chess Club!

In reality, my handwriting and general knowledge improved considerably due to the number of sections of Encyclopaedia Britannica that I had to write out in my innumerable detentions.

* * *

Initially, the first huge shock to my system was being surrounded by GRASS.

My new School had acres of it!

Being a ragamuffin from the backstreets I was used to rows of terraced houses, cobbled alleys and exhaust fumes from the never ending traffic jams on Newport Road.

Now, I was passing detached and semi detached houses, *all with huge gardens*, on my way to School, but the most awe striking site was yet to come.

Acklam Hall itself was magnificent. There was a 'drive' that led to the front of the original manor house, that was more than half a mile long, with no traffic and hardly a hint of Tarmac anywhere.

The original, now defunct, main gate to the manor house, was at the far end of an 'Avenue of Trees', which was about 600 metres long and mainly comprising of tall poplars. Then across a narrow section of road, Hall Drive, which was built after the original owners, the Hustler family, sold the estate to Middlesbrough Council in 1928. Finally, through the School's main gates, down a quarter mile tarmac drive, which was flanked by a pond on one side and the

School's cricket pitches on the other, to arrive at the magnificent 17th century manor house that was now MY Grammar School.

There could not have been a starker contrast between my two formative places of education, unless I'd been sent to study at Eton or Harrow.

On stepping through the impressive stone pillared entrance porch (which of course was out of bounds to pupils) A huge reception room (now our geography room) opened onto an oak, carved spiral staircase which led upstairs to the most magnificent library that you could imagine. I spent many hours studying the magnificent carved ceilings with hanging vines and cherubs surrounding expensive oil paintings in here; (mainly because this was one of the often used sites for my numerous detentions).

The second shock to my system was being surrounded by boys that were more intelligent than me, rather than the muppets at Newport. I was used to being top of the class without trying – now I had to work hard just to keep up.

Also, what was with all this working in silence, and staying in your seat all the time? I'd always been very verbose and hyperactive – although in those days they didn't have a word for my excess of energy

– they just called me a bloody nuisance - and belted me for it.

That didn't work – it only made me even more rebellious, but also more *devious.* I became the class clown and the teachers were often the butt of my humour.

One day I was even given a detention in a Geometry lesson for asking the boy next to me for help with a problem. I was too embarrassed to put my hand up and ask the teacher what a right angle was in the triangle that he'd told us to draw, as every other kid in the class knew, and immediately got down to the task. At Newport School I was the bright lad in the class 'cos I merely knew what a triangle was!!!

Chisel O'Halloran, was the woodwork teacher that all the kids feared. He would often throw a block of wood at a kid for misbehaving or really berate a pupil for doing a job wrong. He got his nickname, however, because, he had been, reputedly, disciplined, himself, for throwing a tool at a boy!

I think he had anger control and blood pressure problems because he would go bright red in the face and start stammering (with a lisp) as he tore strips off some unfortunate child who happened to get the angles on his dovetail joint wrong!

His catchphrase was: "I'll wap this wump of wood awound your head, boy!"

When he victimised me, I went out for revenge.

I was given five hundred lines for being at the wrong end of the classroom – even though he'd sent me there to keep my technical drawing clean of the shavings that my colleague was throwing up on our shared bench.

When I tried to tell him why I was there, he simply stammered "Don't talk back, boy. You've just made it 600 lines ."

"But, sir, you told . . ."

"That's seven hundred lines, and will get bigger every time you open your mouth, boy."

"But . . ."

"Eight hundred lines, boy."

I gave up when we got to a thousand.

Of course I didn't do the lines. This was the one and only time that my mother came to see the Headmaster.

Jack Hurt, was a kindly headmaster, and fortunately didn't live up to his surname. He rarely caned a pupil, and was quite happy to listen to my version of events.

Chisel didn't get his lines, but let me know every subsequent lesson that he wasn't happy with me. If he had just dropped it there, I would have got on with the lesson *despite* him; but he wouldn't let it rest. So I decided to get my own back.

Chisel ran the School bird watching club, and regularly put reports up on the School noticeboard. So after the heat had died down, a few weeks later, I put my own notice up.

On the Annuwal Bird Cwub Outing to Wedcar, We spotted a
> Wobin Wedbwest ,
> Awbertwoss,
> Fwush,
> Budgewigar,
> Empewor Penguin
>   . . . etc.

Unusually, the noticeboard was four deep with pupils laughing their heads off, for a couple of hours before the notice was taken down. Of course, I had disguised my handwriting and didn't tell a soul what I had done, as I was certain to get caned severely for my reprisal, but I really wished that I'd been able to confront Chisel and tell him how he'd caused this reaction.

Later, when I became a teacher myself, although I was a disciplinarian, I tried desperately to listen to a pupil, *before punishing them*. I think that I got this right – but I'm sure some ex-pupils will let me know!

In another lesson, this time Physics, I was taking part in one of my favourite school activities watching a documentary film. The lights were out, and the class was in total silence as we watched "The Making of Margerine" by ICI. Suddenly there was a high pitched squeal from the row in front of me. The lights came on immediately:

"Masters, get out here." The Physics teacher yelled.

"It wasn't me, Sir" I tried to explain.

"Get out here, Masters. I recognised your voice."

"You can't have, Sir, 'cos it wasn't me."

"Don't talk back, Masters, you are only making it worse for yourself."

"It doesn't matter, Sir. You're going to belt me anyway, but I want you to know that it wasn't me.

Mr. Badcock, the physics teacher wasn't going to back down, somebody was going to pay for this outburst, and he didn't care who it was.

As for me, another slippering wasn't going to affect me, one way or another, I was tough enough to take it.

Noel Badcock had different ideas. He coached one of the school rugby teams, and knew I was tough, so he adjusted his punishment.

"Bend over, Masters."

The class roared with laughter, especially Malcom Dewar, whose outburst it had been.

"No, not there, Masters, THERE." He pointed to a position where my head was 2 inches away from the old, corrugated, iron radiator. The nasty b*****d had decided to inflict pain to both ends at once.

WHALLOP – my body flew forward and as expected crashed into the heater. Instantly my knees buckled and I fell into a heap on the floor.

"Get up, Masters, and stop messing about" Badcock yelled, with a hint of panic in his voice.

But I remained, unmoving, in a heap at the foot of the radiator.

Now, Badcock, was really panicking, as he tugged the lifeless body to its feet.
I slumped into a front desk, trying to get my balance. He squeakily ordered "Now get back to your seat, and stop messing about."

I staggered and lurched towards the side isle, past the first two rows of lab benches. The class realised the horror of this situation, and were now totally silent as they watched the spectacle.

I saw my best mate's face, jaw dropped, as he couldn't believe what he was seeing.

So, as I had my back to Noel Badcock and calculated that he couldn't see, I winked at Johnny Craggs, to reassure him that I wasn't hurt and only acting.

Next, as I passed Malc Dewar's seat I whispered to him "I'll get you - at Rugby for that."

Dewar, of course, brought a note for the next three weeks, then after that had to play well enough to work his way back onto the first team pitch. Incredibly, although he was a decent winger, he never played well enough to return to *my* game!

*   *   *

RUGBY! – now that was another HUGE culture shock to the young James Masters. I had never even seen a game of it before going to Acklam. I was a soccer player - Middlesbrough was a FOOTBALL town . Now I was being told that only rugby was played here in the winter and only cricket in the summer. If you were no good at these; ie. couldn't get into one of the four teams that played on the first team or second team pitches, then you were left to your own devices running cross country in the winter or dabbling with athletics in the summer. I hated cross country so I became a rugby player. Also, coming from the rough end of town, I had a point to prove. Even though I was the littlest, at 5 foot 6, on the first team pitch, I had to show these namby pamby snobs that I could more than punch my own weight.

Consequently I tackled everything that moved, ferociously. I wasn't afraid of anyone and could tackle anybody, *except* for one person that is:- Joe Cockburn. Cockburn was a North of England centre, but he also came from my side of the tracks, so that was OK.

A couple of times I had tried to tackle Cockburn in practice and failed so I knew if I was to succeed I would have to go in extra hard to get him down. Most of time he just swatted me away with a big meaty hand-off, but at one particular practice session I went in really aggressively and actually brought him down. I was grinning from ear to ear, when he got up and scowled

"Don't do that again." Then he stamped my hand into the ground with his metal studded boots, just to emphasise his displeasure. I pulled my bloodied hand out of the mud and held it out towards my PE teacher to let him see what had happened but he simply turned his head away. Heaven forbid that he might take this pain in the a***'s side against his pet, star rugby player.

Anyway, I might be tough and brave, but I wasn't stupid – *I didn't do it again!* I'd learnt my lesson weeks before this when in a disagreement with Cockburn, I'd called him 'Pongo' and he erupted; picked me up like a rag doll and hurled me over three desks.

So, I determined then never to pick a fight with him – however, rugby was different, - surely it was part of the game to tackle aggressively. Well, Joe Cockburn didn't think so, and the PE teacher, Don Piggott didn't seem to think so either, so this time *(unusually for me)* I didn't make a fuss over the incident but merely got on with the game, aggressively tackling everyone else.

Rugby became my big passion, but it is the one thing I regret about going to Acklam Hall. If I had have gone to a Soccer School I would have ended up earning my living as a pro. Realistically, I know I wouldn't have played for England, or in the

Premiership, but I was more than capable of achieving a living wage playing for the likes of Hartlepool United or Darlington.

But, that wasn't to be - I was at a rugby only school, so I had to make the most of it. I played at County level at both under 15 and under 19 levels, but that was the height of my achievements in school's competitions.

My Physics teacher, who also played for Middlesbrough, once told me: "You're a good little player, Jimbo, but you're never gonna make it at the top level 'cos you're too small."

So I was caught between a rock and a hard place - my school didn't play the game I was good at and most suited to, but I was too little for the game they forced me to play.

Consequently, I tried to play both games for a long time but if there was a clash I had to opt for rugby first.

On one occasion I made the mistake of telling Pigg that I couldn't play for the School on the following Saturday because my Youth Club had a National Cup match that they wanted me to play in. He went purple in the face and snapped "OK, Jimbo, don't play, but in that case I won't be putting your name forward for County trials, and you won't play for Middlesbrough ever again.

Playing for Middlesbrough was my passion. Brian Ellis was a great team manager of their Colts (under 19 team) that I had played regularly for since I was 15, so that threat really hit home.

*　　　　　*　　　　　*

As mentioned earlier, most of the boys, at Acklam, were much more intelligent than me – but they also had the distinct advantage of being educated in good primary schools that had advanced their education to a greater level than mine at Newport School. Also, at home they were surrounded by books and encyclopaedias which they read regularly.

My home reading comprised mainly of comics. The Beano and the Dandy, led onto Superman and Batman, and my ultimate literary level of Commando war comics or Ladybird books that I loaned from Newport Library. All of them comprised mainly of pictures with short bubble captions or paragraphs. As a result, my reading was slow and poor, especially when compared to the likes of Robert I'Anson, who later became a doctor, and who could speed read. He had finished a chapter in a book while I was still on the second page. Homework for him lasted 30 minutes while I was still struggling with it two hours later (after rugby training or detentions, whichever was on the menu that night).

Rob, once explained his technique to me, whereby he read down the centre of the page, and his peripheral vision took in the rest. I tried it for a month, but my homework was taking EVEN longer as I was constantly back tracking to find the information I'd missed by this method.

So, I went back to plodding along, often handing in homework late, and often getting punished for it.

The bulk of the pupils went on to become doctors, or lawyers, politicians solicitors, pilots, etc. But not all of them achieved greatness. We had our fair share of whacko's too! One such character was Bert Templar.

Like me Bert came from a poor family, but unlike me, he was a genius at Chemistry.

His family background was much poorer than mine. When he went home he had to go straight out to sell newspapers on a street corner in order to pay for his own School uniform as well as the bike that he rode the six miles to School on every day. His trousers were often patched (by him) and he wore sensible heavy boots to School – even in blistering summer heat – because they lasted longer. Consequently the well dressed posh kids made him the butt of their humour, and often played practical jokes on him.

I made the mistake of befriending him – ignoring the fact that he was a nutcase. One day he followed me home from School. Despite my ducking down alleyways and running off route to try to throw him off the scent, he still arrived at my house shortly after me.

I tried to ignore him shouting for me as he pedalled his bike in circles up and down the Street.

"Is that a friend of yours?" Mum asked.

"No!"

"Well he's shouting your name." Mum observed.

"It's Bert Templar, from School, he's a nutter."

"Well he looks frozen stiff. Ask him if he would like a cup of tea."

Totally ignoring the loud NO-O-O that I was shouting, Mum had the front door open and was inviting Bert in.

Bert plonked himself in my Dad's armchair *(good job Dad wasn't in!)* and with a smug look on his face, smiled at me. "Nice place, Jimbo. Lovely to sit in front of a warm fire on a night like this"

"S'alright"

"Would you like a cup of tea, son?" Mum enquired.

"Yes please, Mrs. Masters"

"Would you like sugar?"

"Ooh, yes please, four spoons."

Mum whispered to me *"You can tell he's a Grammar School boy. Lovely manners."*

"It's all an act." I scowled

Totally ignoring me AGAIN, Mum asked "Would you like to stay for Tea, Bert?"

My heart sank.

"It's only Corned Beef Stew, I'm afraid."

"Brilliant, we hardly ever have a hot meal at my house, 'cos we don't have a cooker."

"You don't have an oven?" Mum gasped. "Don't you regularly have hot food then?"

"Oh, we have a gas ring, which we can fry bacon & eggs on, or in cold weather like this I might have some soup. But we never sit down at a table for a meal like this."

"Well you just tuck in, and enjoy," and then to my dismay the dopey woman gave him a larger portion than me!!! *We were never going to get rid of him at this rate. He'll be coming round every night!*

Bert gulped the food down before I'd finished half of mine, and Mum said, "Well you seemed to enjoy that"

"It was lovely Mrs. Masters"

"Would you like a dessert?"

"Oh yes please, what is it?"

"Only banana custard, I'm afraid."

"Sounds great. I've never eaten a banana before."

"Never eaten a banana? Well I'm sure you'll enjoy them. I'll put extra on your plate."

Templar smiled with his creepiest expression, I put my head in my hands and stared down at my empty plate. Not only was Mum falling for his false politeness, but he was eating more of my favourite food than I was getting.

There was no other way for it, I had to UNbefriend him.

Bert came round to my house on a further three occasions before he eventually got the message.

I joined the posh boys in teasing him. On one particular occasion we all went illegally into the School orchard (a week's detention for being caught there) and we were throwing snowballs at each other.

"Let's have a slide on the pond" Ted suggested.

"The ice is probably not thick enough" Don said.

"Well let's test it," Ted replied. "Who's the heaviest, if it'll take his weight, we'll all be alright."

Everybody looked at Bert Templar, who then admitted "I suppose I'm the biggest" and gingerly tested the ice at the edge of the pond.

The plan had worked.

"It's no good testing the edge," Don said, "we'll be sliding across the middle."

Bert edged precariously further and further forward, testing with his big heavy boots as he went. When he reached the middle, somebody shouted "Now" and we all picked up the rocks and logs that we had scoured for on our way into the Orchard, and began braying the ice at the edges with them. Sure enough the ice cracked, and Bert went down like the Titanic.

Then we all scarpered in case he got out.

We could hear "You b******s, over our shoulders as we giggled away, "I'm gonna put every one of you in hospital when I get out of here."

I glanced over my shoulder and could see Bert up to his waist in the freezing and stinking pond, trying desperately to get a grip on the ice to haul himself out. I wasn't going to stop running, as Templar was well known for his temper, and for beating up boys who upset him. I just hoped he'd remembered my previous friendship and went easy on me.

Now all this seemed a bit harsh on the nutty Bert, but we all knew the *real* Mr. Templar, an example of which was displayed the following summer.

Again in the 'out of bounds' orchard, Templar was showing us all some of his tricks. Bert, the chemistry genius had made some nitro-glycerine at home and carried it to School in a Lowcocks lemonade bottle. God knows what carnage would have developed if it had exploded as it joggled up and down in his haversack when he rode his bike to School!

Now we all gathered around as he was pouring the liquid into small hollowed out pools at the base of some sapling trees. Then he stood back and threw a rock at the liquid, after a couple of misses he hit dead centre. The nitro exploded and sent the small tree upwards like an Exocet missile. Then, as we moved on to the next tree, somebody shouted "Prefects" and we all scarpered in different directions, but to no avail. The prefects who had obviously heard the explosions, surrounded the orchard before they closed in on us. We were all caught in their trap, except for Don who thought that in all the confusion, if he climbed a tree he might not be noticed. Unfortunately for him the eagle-eyed Head Prefect *had* spotted him and quickly ran forward to grab his ankle. "Get down from there," the prefect shouted, "you've got a week's detention."

Don sheepishly showed his face to Henry Pugh, his older brother, who was also Head Boy.

"YOU, - You!!! Just wait till our mother finds out."

Don was led away, pointlessly protesting to his older brother, but to no avail.

Both Don and Henry later became GP's. Their mother must have been proud.

Unfortunately, the last I heard of Bert Templar was a report of a court case in the Evening Gazette. He had become a student at Durham, and to supplement his grant was selling the drug LSD, that he had made in the College labs, around the local nightclubs.

He swapped Durham University for a stretch in Durham Jail.

*   *   *

As you will have gathered, in my teens all I was interested in was sport. School work wasn't as easy, so I avoided it like the plague - unfortunately now the time was drawing near when I was to leave school.

Don't get me wrong, I didn't mind hard work, as long as I saw the point of it; that meant History was out, so was French and to be honest at that age so were most school subjects. I saw the light with Maths and English, but really all I wanted to do and work at was SPORT. I would just play, or train, at it all day and every day (when I wasn't on detention).

But now, back in the real world, the time was drawing near when I had to leave school.

I had been given a time and date for my Careers Interview.

The dreaded day came.

I entered the room to see a grey man in a grey suit who asked me what I wanted to do with my life.

"Sport," I replied, "Anything to do with Sport."

"Right then," he said, looking down at some very thin notes, "You couldn't consider professional sport, because you are not good enough. Then there's P.E. teaching *but* you wouldn't get into college. So that just leaves the Army."

I nodded.

"Next !"

The interview lasted all of about four minutes.

A few days later I was standing outside of the Army Careers Office in Middlesbrough. The office next door was the RAF s careers office so I acquired some forms from them also.

The RAF became favourite for my talents because they seemed to be put less emphasis on discipline and drilling, but also, and more importantly, I suspected it was less likely that I'd be sent to serve in Northern Ireland with them! (At that time the war against the IRA was still in full swing and I had no intention of being part of it).

If I was going to be sent to Ireland, I wanted to be flying above everything with the Brylcreem boys, not down on the streets getting buckets of urine poured over my head from angry residents!

I had never dreamt of becoming a teacher, but I did consider going to Art College after school – Farnham was my choice as they had a good reputation in ceramics, but the RAF won out because sport was my main passion, and sport could only be pursued intensively while I was young. If I found I'd made a mistake, I could always take up Pottery when I was older, but it wouldn't work the other way around.

So, it was sorted, the Brylcreem boys for me!. A few months of basic training, and then a posting to a base where I would spend most of my time playing sport and doing as little work as possible.

That's how *I* saw it, anyway.
My only worry was that the RAF might not see it quite like that.

Then there was still the discipline! I wasn't too sure if I could take it.

I puzzled over this one for what seemed like several weeks, but in reality was probably closer to minutes. Then I had it! A total change of direction - Real work!

I'd get a proper job! Forget about playing around and enjoying myself. Get down to some real work, and earn some big money: - Accountancy!

I was good at Maths, so why not use it to earn loads of money?

I wrote off for interviews.

Williamson's replied.

They grilled me intensively one afternoon, and to my surprise, offered me a job!!!

Sports car and mansion here I come!

I took a short holiday and started working for them on a cold grey Monday morning.

Mum had bought me a brand new, shiny, grey suit, from Niman's with a 'Provie' cheque, for the big day. It itched like mad, so I went into work with some pyjama bottoms under the trousers. I looked like something out of 'The Godfather' - Beautiful Italian tailoring, close fitting with small lapels, in shiny light grey material.

As I entered the grey premises on this particularly grey day, I looked like a spiv who had accidently walked in on an undertakers' convention.

I was tea boy/mail boy for one week, including a sick day, before I plucked up the courage to tell them I was quitting.

I think both parties were relieved.

Mum wasn't too happy, but felt a lot better when I announced that School had accepted me back into the sixth form, and that I was going to do 'A' levels and then go into the RAF as a Physical Training *Officer.*

Dad wanted me to join the Army just like he had.

"I don't know why your messing about with these A levels – you should join the Army *now*. They'll make a man of you"

"Just like they did for you," I quipped back, "No thanks, I want better than that"

"Well you're just wasting your time. You should be bringing money into this house. *I was working* when I was fourteen."

"And look where it got you"

"You cheeky little . . ."

"Leave him alone!" My mother, as always, jumped in to defend me, "he's going to be more than a van driver. He's going to university."

I just smiled sweetly at my mum, and then glared at Dad. I didn't like to burst her bubble, but with 'A' levels in Art and

Pottery, – I definitely wasn't going to be accepted at university.

My 'O'level results were published soon afterwards and all my efforts bore little fruit. I passed one out of seven. So in the sixth form was re-sitting 'O' levels as well as doing 'A' levels

That was a BIG turning point in my life. It was the last time that I ever failed an exam, whether academic, driving test, or anything!. Suddenly, Jack the Lad became Jack the Scholar - well for a short time at least. A leopard can t completely change his spots, but I did manage to camouflage them for just long enough.

*   *   *

The teachers at Acklam Hall, certainly had a huge influence on my development into adulthood. The two above mentioned teachers taught me how NOT to do it, and I was determined to be a better teacher than them, but of course not all teachers were bad. I had a wonderful form teacher called Ken Midgely who talked to us compassionately. He understood that we were only kids, growing up, excitable, with an excess of energy to use, but he also made it quite clear that he wouldn't put up with any misbehaviour. The main difference, though, was that he asked us to behave, and we responded. I based a lot of my future attitude as a teacher on his approach. I even borrowed one of his catchphrases when I confronted a pupil that was pushing things a bit too far. I initially implored a pupil to behave, but if they didn't I would then fix them with an icy glare and ask "Are you trying to upset me?"

99% of the time this worked, as the then panicking pupil suspected that this veiled question hid a far greater punishment, if ignored, and generally squeaked a reply of "No, Sir," before settling down into compliance.

However, the one teacher who had the most influence on me was a wonderful giddy lady called Georgia Naylor, my ceramics teacher. The very nature of the subject meant that as we prepared clay, or threw pots, (Yes – I know - I have an A level in Pottery *and I was a rugby player!!!* - more about that later) we would have plenty of opportunities to chat - about anything and everything. It was the best General Studies/Psychology/Sociology/Philosophy class that any misunderstood 'A' level student could ever wish for. I was very opinionated *(still am)* and very hot headed, which often got me into bother. Georgia would often calm me down and explain that I couldn't go around always trying to put the world right, and would reason with me saying "You know, Jim, everything in life is not black and white. There are little grey areas to most things."

I've tried to carry this philosophy throughout life and take a balanced view on most things except one. When you are teaching *young* kids they NEED black and white. They need to know that No means no, and that Yes is a promise that you don't break. Too many teachers have a grey flexible approach to how they deal with children, and this doesn't work. (except in Mrs Naylor's case)

Kids need to know where the line is drawn in the sand. If you shift this line, every day, they are confused, especially if they are then punished for doing something that only the day before was acceptable.

This doesn't mean that you need to be nasty with the kids, it means that you let them know where the boundaries are and that if they cross them then nicely correct their error by asserting "I asked you not to do that. Are you trying to upset me?"

Try it. It works.

Thanks Ken.
Thanks Georgia.

*   *   *

Georgia's calming influence and debates worked wonders on me, I was a reformed character, but unfortunately many other members of staff had long memories and dealt with me as the rebellious pupil that I HAD been in my first four years.

One such teacher was Alan Robshaw, the Head of Art, and my 'A' level tutor. (I know, 'A' level Art and Rugby???)

I almost gave Georgia a heart attack one day when Robshaw, came storming into the pottery room and yelled at her "What do you know about this student's 'A' level project being damaged yesterday?"

"Nothing"

"Well it was done in your room."

"Well I don't know anything about it because . . ."

"You are trying to tell me that you don't know what goes on in your own room?

"Excuse me Mr.Robshaw," I said in her defence, "It was Mrs. Naylor's day off yesterday."

"What's this got to do with you?" Robshaw screamed at me, the veins sticking out on his purple forehead. "Just keep your nose out."

That was it, a red mist descended over my eyes as I yelled back, "Well, YOU are totally out of order, yelling at Mrs, Naylor in front of a full class of children!"

"Get out! Get out of this class, I'll see you outside."

"Fine by me" I shouted back as I strode out of the room.

By this time, Georgia was panicking, as she could see the fury in my face. She thought that I was going to punch her Head of Art, - but she needn't have worried.

In the corridor, Robshaw again screeched at me splattering my face with saliva and his bad cigarette breath.

"How dare you, How dare you talk to me like that?"

"Oh, so it is OK for you to yell and scream at another teacher in front of a full class, but not alright when somebody does it to you!"

"I am Head of Department and . . ."

"That doesn't make it right"

"You insolent little upstart."

"That doesn't make me wrong"

"Until you apologise for this outburst you will not set foot in my classroom again" he said, as he turned on his heels to walk back to his sanctuary.

So that was the end of my 'A' level art classes, because he never did receive an apology.

In hindsight, I should have gone to the Headmaster and reported Robshaw's behaviour, as well as demanding reinstatement on my 'A' level course, but as a teenager you don't think of these things. At that moment in time I was only too pleased to rid myself of him.

Anyway, Mrs. Naylor taught me more about Art in our daily sessions, than Robshaw did in his 2 hour intensive A level lessons. – BUT the main thing that she gave me was confidence in myself. My aspirations had been low mainly because I was surrounded by other students that were much cleverer than me, and also by constantly being put down by other teachers. Bill Harrison, my English teacher, once told me that I was wasting my time attending English lessons, as it was like a foreign language to me. I hope he's reading this - my FIFTH book. OK, so it's not Dickens or Shakespeare *(I never intended that)* but it ain't a foreign language either (please excuse the grammar Mr. Harrison !)

Before Mrs. Naylor tutored me through 'O' level Ceramics, and then eventually 'A' level. my aspiration on leaving school was to join the RAF.

But, as I wrote in the previous book in this trilogy, FATE, had different ideas.

I was in the pottery room, throwing some simple vases and mugs that I was going to sell at one of the shops in Middlesbrough, when Mrs. Naylor asked me if I was busy.

"Not really," I replied.

"Well could you show these four second years how to throw a pot on the wheel, for me?"

How could I refuse?

I showed them how to prepare the clay so that there are no air bubbles in it, how to centre it on the wheel, then how to pull it up into a basic cylinder which could then become a mug or vase. Then, it was time for them to have a go. Taking turns each on our two electric wheels - the clay went everywhere. The kids laughed and giggled as their formative cylinders repeatedly flopped and collapsed over their arms, as they overworked the clay. Suddenly the bell went. We were having such good fun that we hadn't noticed the time. The kids quickly threw off their aprons and pulled their blazers on over their gooey arms and hands and sprinted out of the door in order to avoid a probable detention for being late for their next lesson. Of course I was left with the mess on TWO wheels to clean up, but I didn't mind, I'd had a great time. Mrs. Naylor saw my predicament and came over to help.

"You know, James," she said.

Being called James, by most teachers, normally meant I was in trouble, but the smile on Georgia's face told me that this was not the case. But it did mean that she had something serious to say.

"D'you know, I watched you showing those kids how to throw, and you did a great job. I also noticed how much you, and they, enjoyed it. You had a very easy style with them. You are a natural teacher. Have you ever thought about going into teaching?"

I didn't reply, I just fell about bellowing with laughter.

Only Mrs. Naylor could have said or thought that.

All of the other members of staff at Acklam Hall would have recommended her for St. Luke's Mental Hospital for even thinking that.

But the seeds *were* sown.

Chapter 3

A Different Boy

Acklam Hall was also life changing in many other ways. It presented opportunities to me that wouldn't have been available at most other schools.

There were numerous clubs and activities going on every evening.

I've already mentioned the 'Bird Club' which I didn't partake in, but I did join the Chess Club - learnt the game, and eventually made the team – *only once* – I played eighth board against Ripon Grammar School, but as I made the School rugby team soon afterwards my priorities changed and my afterschool activities were now totally dominated by rugby training (and detentions) so there was no time left for chess, or the choir that I'd been chosen for!

Another activity that I took part in that I will be forever grateful for was the Duke of Edinburgh's Award. This opened up new horizons and adventures for me that, again, were life changing. I would recommend this for any school pupil, and every parent should actively encourage it.

I also think it should be a part of every school's curriculum and not just an afterschool club as it was at Acklam.

Through it, I learned First Aid; at which I had to gain the St.John Ambulance Basic certificate in order to pass my Bronze DofE, and I also chose to study Fire Safety in order to pass my Silver award. The Fire Safety Award necessitated attending Middlesbrough Fire Station and learning the main types and causes of fire and how to put them out using the correct type of extinguisher.

Both of these, above, courses have been invaluable throughout my life. That's why I believe that it should be included in every school's curriculum. They are much more relevant to the 21st century than many of the school subjects that I was forced to study.

The DofE also obliged us to take up new recreational activities. For me this was orienteering for my bronze award, and rock climbing for my silver.

As a 'townie' I had never really experienced the natural beauty that was right on my doorstep – the North Yorkshire Moors; - and I will always be grateful to Acklam Hall and the DofE award for presenting me with this opportunity.

In the summer, out of rugby season, I spent almost every weekend camping out on the 'Moors'.

Orienteering was a complete novelty for me, not only learning how to use a map and compass, but also discovering fantastic villages and sites in North Yorkshire (plus many more lesser known interesting ones when we got lost!)

My group of new friends, who gradually became lifelong buddies consisted of Don Pugh, (who later went on to become a doctor), Ted White, (who, like me became a teacher) and Johhny Craggs (who became a Quantity Surveyor). We all played for Middlesbrough Rugby Club as well as the School team, so we were all very competitive - between each other, as well as with other groups. Consequently while we were learning we always wanted to be the leader, and beat each other at tasks set, but when it came to the organised competition at the end of the course, it went without saying that no other team would be allowed to beat us.

Imagine our horror then, in our final test, on a six mile orienteering course, when we made a mistake and went the wrong way. By the time we had corrected ourselves, with only one mile to go, we could see another team about a quarter of a mile ahead of us, striding out purposefully across the ridge of a hill towards the finish. The only way we could beat them was to take a short cut, and RUN. So we studied the map and decided that their route along the ridge of a crescent shaped hill was much longer than if we went directly to the finish down into the valley along the narrow track, skirted on both sides by marshland, and up the other side of the valley to the finish on the peak of the hill.

So, with our compasses and maps firmly clenched in our hands, and our heavy rucksacks set on our backs we set off at a fast jog down into the valley. We were definitely gaining on them. They saw us and were obviously worried as they picked up their own pace, but they must have fallen about in hysterics when they saw Johnny, our then leader, up to his waist in the bog, as he missed the track, and the rest of us splashing about in the mire, as we attempted to drag him out before he completely disappeared.

We made the finishing line still in an annoying second place, exhausted, soaked up to the waist with filthy stinking mud and the butt of much merriment.

The orienteering set us up nicely though for the toughest test of the Award: – the Expedition. To pass this section of the award we had to walk 30 miles in five days through the countryside carrying everything we needed to survive, on our backs.

We also had to go in a minimum sized group of four and only in the Spring or Summer on the NY moors, as it was considered 'wild' country and much too hazardous in the winter months.

This was going to be a doddle for our group. We were all experienced map readers, walkers and campers. All of us, except Ted, had chosen Rock Climbing as our 'new' hobbies so we were out on the 'Moors, mainly at the Wainstones, practicing nearly every weekend. We regularly 'camped out,' even in winter, not even bothering to take a tent. We just took a rope, some beans, eggs and bacon, equipment to cook on and most invaluable; our arctic sleeping bags. At the Wainstones especially we would just sleep under the rocks, after having windproofed the sides of our accommodation with smaller rocks and grass sods – leaving just enough space to enter (which we then covered from the inside with our rucksacs), after crawling through to reach our sleeping area. Toastie warm and comfortable. We did this many times without any problem, except for the time when I awoke from a deep slumber, forgot where I was and sat up, cracking my head, hard, on the rock ceiling, immediately putting myself back into a deeper slumber!

Due to the extreme experiences above, we expected that the Expedition was going to be so simple for these experienced, hardy, rock climbers. We had arranged with our DofE organiser to take the final test the following summer, but first we needed a practice. Completely ignoring the fact that expeditions weren't allowed on the 'Moors' in winter, (after all it was going to be *so* easy for us), we planned (without the organiser knowing) a practice in February.

We all met up at Craggsy's house, and planned the route meticulously. We sorted out who would carry which pieces of group equipment in their rucksacs, as well as their own personal equipment and emergency rations. The tent was divided up, the camping stoves, pots & pans, torches, etc. shared out. But I don't think anybody took spare clothes or soap. (That tent, after 5 days and thirty miles of rough hiking, was going to smell *lovely*). Then we each made a route map, with approximate timings, and another emergency one for our parents – so if they needed to contact us during the expedition (or if we didn't arrive home at the arranged time) they knew where we would be (*in theory*).

So, when the chosen February date came around, we set off from our beloved starting point in Great Broughton. This time, however, we walked past the Wainstones, and took a horseshoe shaped route eventually expecting to end up, 5 days later, at Guisborough, where Craggsy's dad had arranged to pick us all up in his car.

We warned him to bring a peg for his nose !

As you would expect, when you totally ignore sense and warnings about practicing at this time of year, fate steps in; so that when we set off - it was snowing heavily.

We all thought little of this, in fact, it made the countryside look even prettier and an added bonus was that we didn't have to search out and check streams for water – we simply melted snow. (except the yellow stuff!)

In high spirits, we began our trek. The snow, though, was covering and hiding footpaths, and making the going tougher. No problem, however, as we were all experienced map readers (as you obviously realised from the orienteering competition) so we cracked on. Despite numerous arguments and discussions regarding the route we were taking, we made the first three nights pitches accurately, and on time. By the fourth night the heavy snow had now become a blizzard. We had planned to camp on the public land right next to the river in Castleton, which, despite the appalling weather, we made, again, accurately and on time.

Pitching the tent, however, was a nightmare in the blizzard. Everytime we tried to peg it down, the wind filled it like an air balloon and tried to carry it, and us, away with it. The snowflakes were getting in our eyes and made it hard to see what we were doing, but between the four of us we eventually pegged our 'arctic' classified tent down and doubly secured the guy ropes. After all, we didn't want it to be flying away during the night as we were taking some well deserved sleep.

We ensured (as you should) that the back of the tent was facing the wind. In no time at all, the back and one of the sides was thickly covered in a layer of snow. As night began to fall, we made ourselves a warm mug of tomato soup, took our waterproofs off and snuggled deeply into our arctic sleeping bags still fully clothed. We laughed and joked and told stories to each other, but pretty soon the warmth and tiredness of our exertions started to get to us and we all, at probably only about 8 pm, started to drift off to sleep.

That sleep didn't last long!

"Who's in there?" a gruff voice bellowed, as a torch beam played across the sides of our tent. "Who's in there?"

We all sat up startled, and Don shouted out "There are four of us." Hoping to deter any would-be robber with our numerical advantage. "WHO are you?"

"I'm, PC Davies, the village bobby – . What on earth are you doing camping out in this weather?"

At this point, Don risked partly unzipping the front of the tent and popping his head out. Sure enough, there was the Castleton village bobby, hair and helmet thick with snow, holding on to a torch in one hand and his regulation village bobby's bike in the other. "We're doing the Duke of Edinburgh's Award."

"IN THIS WEATHER??? You must be crazy!

Is there anybody coming out to check on you tonight?"

"No we're just doing this as a practice."

"Well, you'll freeze to death out here. I'll tell you what, it's a lot warmer in the police station, if nobody's checking on you, why don't you all come and sleep in my cells?"

"Thanks for the offer." Don replied, but we're really all right. We've slept out in worse than this. We've all got arctic sleeping bags and warm clothes. Do you want to come in for a cuppa before *you* freeze to death?"

No thanks, lad, I've still got the rest of my round to do, besides I'm covered in snow, I'd get all of your tent wet. Thanks for the offer. If you change your mind, the offers still open. The Police Station is just over there," pointing to his left, "400 yards away."

"Thanks, but I'm sure we'll be alright."

"OK, goodnight." And with a cheery wave PC Plod turned his bike towards the Station, and went on his way.

We saw his torch beam shine on the sides of our tent twice more in the early hours of that night, and the next morning, and, just as we were frying breakfast, he turned up again.

This time Ted had his head out of the tent, as he tended to the camping stoves.

"Well, you lads survived the night alright then" PC Davies said.

"We told you we'd be OK.

Do want a cuppa this time"

"Aye, lad, I will this time."

So Ted quickly threw away the cold remnants of his brew, washed the mug out and replenished it for our friendly copper."

"Thanks, son. So what's your plans, now, then?"

"Well as soon as we've had breakfast, we'll pack all this gear away and then it's our last days slog into Guiborough, where we are getting picked up."

"Well rather you than me in this snow. And is that it then – you've passed the course?"

"Not really, this is just a practice. The real thing takes place next summer"

"Well, if you can do it in these conditions, you will pass in the summer, no problem."

"Exactly what we thought," Ted replied.

Unfortunately, it wasn't as easy as that, because when the Summer came around, Ted had glandular fever on the planned date of the Expedition. The rest of us couldn't do it without him, and by the time Ted recovered there wasn't another block of five days that we could all put together until the winter again.

So despite all of our efforts, passing all the other categories in the Award, we all fell short of gaining our Silver Awards by failing to complete what should have been the easiest part for us.

No regrets, though, the experience and the fun of it all was really worth it.

As I said earlier I think all parents should encourage their kids to take part in the DofE. It is invaluable for the life skills that the children learn.

Also, again to reiterate what I have previously suggested, I think that the Duke of Edinburgh's Award should be part of every school's curriculum, and gaining a Bronze award should be considered by employers and exam boards as the equivalent of a GCSE – the Silver award on a par with an 'O' level, and obviously, then, the Gold award would be equivalent to a GCE 'A' level.

*　　　　*　　　　*

I've always been keen on pupils learning life skills at school rather than some of the subjects that I found irrelevant in my studies. This belief led me to teaching Motor Vehicle Studies whilst I was at Hawksmount School. I believed then, and still do, that far too many of our children are hazardous on our increasingly busier roads, and far too many die needlessly at far too young an age.

Throughout my teaching career I have personally known five pupils who died in motorbike crashes. This, plus my own experiences on a motorbike, prompted me to teach MVS, hopefully to save some lives.

This interest was prompted, in no small way, by my own life threatening experiences on the first day that I rode a motor scooter.

I had bought a Lambretta as soon as I turned sixteen, for the princely sum of ten pounds (probably the equivalent of £120 nowadays).

It was a sky blue LDA. *Classy*

Classy, because the A at the end of its name stood for Automatic – so no pumping the starter pedal up and down on the side of the bike for young James, no sir, I just turned the key and the ignition fired up immediately.

Well, in theory.

In reality I spent more time running that bike up and down Laycock Street, (bump starting it), than I did starting it with the key! But it was fun.

I chose a scooter, because in those days I was a Mod. I didn't wear a parka, and have stacks of mirrors and lights all across the front of my Lambretta, but I did wear flared trousers, centre-parted and backcombed my hair, and listened to the Small Faces and Spencer Davis as I hung out with all my mates at the Excel Bowling Alley in Middlesbrough every weekend.

So, a scooter it was. The other advantage of buying a scooter was that one of my friends, who lived six doors away, and was in the year above me at Acklam Hall, had been riding a scooter for a year by then, and had promised to teach me how to ride it as soon as I'd bought one..

Big mistake. BIG BIG MISTAKE.

David Jay's idea of teaching me to ride the scooter was just to tell me to follow him.

In those days (and I'm really, really pleased the laws have changed) we could just buy a motorbike at age sixteen, tax and insure it, and then take to the road without any lessons or experience.

So that's what prompted David Jay's idea of instruction.

He showed me how to switch on with the bike in neutral, showed me where the brakes were and then said "Just pull the clutch in with this lever, twist the grip to select first gear and then you're off.

Right then:- Follow me and we'll find somewhere quiet to practice."

His idea of 'somewhere quiet' was the old disused Aerodrome at Thornaby – a FOUR mile ride - *on main roads!!!*

He had passed the eleven plus just like me, and gone to grammar school!!! So, it was unbelievable that he was so stupid!

Remarkably, so had I, but I was still daft enough to follow him. Naively, at that age, I thought he knew what he was doing.

So, off we went, Dizzy Dave, I think, was trying to impress with his ability and expertise, so drove much TOO fast for me. Desperate not to lose him, I thrashed the bike in order to keep up. He was probably doing 40 down Laycock Street when he came to the right angled corner of Carlow Street. He slowed down, leaned his scooter over and took the turn easily. As for me, on the first corner I'd ever taken on my scooter, it was all too fast and extreme. I didn't lean over far enough, ran off the road, mounted the pavement and the drove down the pedestrian walkway for about 40 metres before a gap in the parked cars, allowed me to come off again. I had, *scarily*, travelled past about a dozen or so front doors at 30 miles an hour. - If anybody had stepped out I would, almost certainly have killed them.

Meanwhile, Dopey Dave was way out in front and hadn't seen a thing of this. He continued to pull away at 40 mph.

Totally shaken by this incident, I dropped my speed down to 20 mph, and let him go. After a few minutes, he obviously glanced behind, saw I wasn't there and came back to collect me. As soon as he saw me, he simply waved, U-turned his bike and gestured for me to follow, and sped off at 40 miles an hour AGAIN.

Having learned my lesson I gradually increased my speed up to thirty, but this time was determined to go no faster. Dave would just have to come back for me again, and maybe*, just maybe*, after he has come back a few times, he would get the message.

Besides, my bike was struggling to stay with him, and was making a funny high pitched noises (probably overheating too) as during my brief lesson before we set off, Dopey Dave hadn't explained about changing gears, and I travelled all the way to Thornaby (4 miles) in first gear!!!

When we got to the Aerodrome, I told him what had happened, and the funny noise my bike was making, and I think he realised his mistakes, because he then instructed me on how to change gear, and had me practice braking, and taking numerous corners.

After about half an hour of this, he decided that was enough. I was an expert now; it was time to go home.

Obviously learning nothing from the previous trip and my moaning, he set off at 40 miles an hour again.

I, of course, travelled slowly behind him at between 20 and 30 mph. This time I knew the route back home, so didn't need to be on his tail. David kept circling back for me, but still didn't take the hint. I suppose he hoped that I would speed up to keep up with him, but I just kept it steady. As we turned out of Burlam Road, the next stretch down Roman Road was straight, and almost home, so I increased my speed to 30 mph to stay on his tail. But, then, he suddenly went off the expected route and threw a right hander, to go down St. Barnabas Road. Not expecting this, I leaned my bike over later than him, and a flurry of sparks told me that I had leaned it over too far. The scooter, crashed and skidded in a cacophony of sparks and grinding metal, down Barny's Rd., whilst my body went straight on down Roman Road.

This is where, eventually, I *was* lucky, because although I had been thrown off my bike, I landed on my backside, and was travelling on my rump at thirty mph. I felt the tarmac ripping at my jeans, then shredding my underpants, and finally grinding down the flesh of my backside. I couldn't stop this happening, because my body, unlike the scooter, wasn't fitted with brakes. However, although I know this doesn't sound too lucky up to now, *it was*, because I hadn't landed heavily on my shoulder or arms, and broken any bones. Also I was skidding along in an almost seated position, so that when I inevitably hit the kerb, it was feet first, not with my hip or shoulder which both would have definitely shattered. I was able to jam my feet against the kerb, slowing me down considerably. The momentum, however, still turned my body over, in a somersault, so that I was going quite slowly when my curled up body hit the wall of Middlesbrough General Hospital; only twenty five metres from the Ambulance Station. *What better place to have your first crash?*

Fortunately, I didn't need their services. I simply limped over to my scooter whose engine was still running. Turned it off and then kicked the right hand side running board straight, and was able to ride it again.

David, meanwhile had once again circled back to see what had happened. I couldn't be bothered talking to him. I just called him a 'f*****g idiot, jumped on the scooter and drove home at 15 miles an hour.

I never spoke to David Jay again:-
I didn't fancy any more near death experiences.

When I got home, I limped down the passage to the living room. I opened the door, but didn't step in. I just said "Hiya" to my Mum, desperately trying not to show any pain on my face.

"You're in early, something wrong?" she asked.

"No, I forgot to take any money out with me, I need some petrol" Then I closed the door and dragged myself up the stairs to my bedroom. There, I gingerly took my ruined jeans off and examined the injury. It looked like a large very raw sirloin steak.

I took some lint, Savlon, and adhesive tape from the bathroom cabinet (already my DofE first aid course paying dividends) and padded out my rear. Then I delicately pulled a pair of baggy tracksuit bottoms over the injury, and went downstairs again.

"Right I'm off out" I shouted to Mum through a half open door.

"Where you going?"

I gave the usual teenage reply, "Just out, on me scooter,. See ya"

"Bye, be careful." Mum shouted back, as I shut the front door behind me.

I then let out a huge blast of breath as I congratulated myself in pulling that one off. If my Mother had discovered the truth of why I had popped home she would have made me sell my scooter, and banned me from riding another. This would have deprived me of a lot of fun, and mobility, but would have also saved me from a lot of (less serious) incidents.

The above incident(s) was one of the major reasons why I am now the proud owner of both the Cleveland Motor Cycle Proficiency Certificate and the Schools Traffic Education Programme Certificate. AND why I went on to teach Motor Vehicle Studies at school.

*   *   *

As explained in the previous story, my DofE first aid certificate came in useful in that incident (and many others throughout my life).

However, the DofE was also responsible for introducing me to Rock Climbing, which I took up as my required new hobby.

I loved it being out in the wilds, most summer weekends. I should have been born a country boy, not a townie as I was, but through Rock Climbing I was determined to make up for lost time now.

I became very proficient at this craft, and studied guide books of all of the local rock faces, always wanting to attempt the most severe climbs at these outcrops.

This ability caused me to be over confident, on a couple of occasions, which almost killed me: - but I survived, and learned, yet another lesson, the hard way.

Lesson One: *you should never climb a rockface that you haven't seen before without a top rope.*

It was a glorious summer's day, and all of our pals had decided to meet up at the peak of Roseberry Topping. We all made our own way there, so leaving my scooter in the car park of the Kings Head in Newton Under Roseberry, (I was sure that we would be having a drink there later), I set off for the summit.

As I neared the top I saw a very inviting rock face that I didn't know existed. It looked just as easy to climb this as to skirt around it on the longer footpath to the summit.

So I stopped and studied it in detail. It was approximately forty feet high it had very easy handholds and footholds all the way to its peak. I studied it carefully a second time, just to double check the route I was going to take, Once I was happy that everything was straightforward, I set off up it.

Sure enough it was a doddle, I climbed 35 feet with no problems whatsoever, but the final handhold – which looked so easy from the ground - was much too far to stretch. I couldn't make it, so I looked around for an alternative – NOTHING. I was in a pickle here; - could I just climb back down – NO. The problem in attempting this is that your eyes are at the top of your body and you have to lean well away from the rock face to see past your feet to find where your next foothold is. Almost impossible to do. So, I looked to my left and right for a possible traverse.

Nothing on the left, but on the right there was a big ledge which led to an easy scramble to the summit – *but* it was six feet away, and I could only stretch my arms to reach about four feet. So that was ruled out.

I went back to examining the face for easier alternatives but there were none.

Panic and tiredness were setting in, and my body started to shake. Through my now fairly extensive experience of rock climbing, I recognised these signs, I was about to peel off and plummet 35 feet to almost certain serious injury or even death. There was only one thing for it. In an enormous explosion of adrenalin fuelled effort I hurled my body to my right in an attempt to reach that ledge that was six feet away – if I missed it or slipped, I was probably dead!

Fortunately, (as you know 'cos I'm writing this), I didn't die. I made it, and desperately clung to the ledge. My next worry was also unfounded because my hands didn't lose their grip as I got there, and I held on like a limpet, for a relieved few seconds, before frantically scrambling over the top.

I needed a change of underpants, but I got there, - AND NEVER EVER

CLIMBED WITHOUT A TOP ROPE, again!

Lesson Number Two: (This time I did have a top rope), and it was another glorious sunny morning at the Wainstones.

I'd gone there with my usual rock climbing mates, Johnny & Don, and we had had a great days climbing on the Saturday, but they were still in their sleeping bags snoring away at 7 am. It was too glorious a Sunday morning to waste lying in bed, - I was ready to go! I had always been an early riser, and this beautiful sunny weather just made me want to get up & start climbing again.

I went up a side path to the top of the rocks, and felt like I was in Heaven. I just sat there, eating my cornflakes, in the sunshine, dangling my legs over the 50 foot drop of 'Main Wall' with 'The Sphinx' on my right, and 'Ling Buttress' on my left, looking out over the patchwork quilt of fields that was the Vale of Teesside.

What better way to start a Sunday could anyone have?

Rule number two in rock climbing – never climb in less than a three (in case there's an accident) If this happens one person should stay with the victim whilst the other one goes for help.

But that didn't apply to this case, 'cos I wasn't going to climb!

I was going to abseil – what could be the danger in that?

We'd finished the day before by abseiling down Ling Buttress, so I knew exactly what to expect, where to belay the rope, the layout of the face, etcetera, etcetera. And, as we'd had no problems the day before, what could possibly go wrong?

So with Craggsy and Pugsly still snoring away, I quietly picked the rope up from outside our grotto and headed for Ling. I belayed the rope to a solid rock at the top of the Buttress, ran it through my Karabiner, which was attached to my figure of eight harness, and walked backwards to the top of the rockface. At the edge I took a firm grip of the rope; my right hand above me, my left hand holding the rope below the 'Krab.' This was going to jam forward if I needed to stop in an emergency for any reason.

Now came the part that scares most novices stiff, I had to lean out from the top until my body was at a right angle to the face, so that my shoes would grip the rock, and my legs could function properly.

A little at a time I slowly fed the rope out and leaned back. 20 degrees – 40 degrees – 60 degrees – 80 degrees out and then T-W-A-N-G. My feet flew upwards, my head shot down, the harness slipped up around my ankles and I was plummeting towards the rocks below at a rapid rate of knots. I'd dropped about thirty feet before I gained my composure and realised that I had to slow myself down somehow before I crashed into the jagged rocks just twenty feet below me.

The rope was now rapidly whistling past my left ear, fortunately it hadn't snapped which had been my first thought, but merely snagged on a small rock at the top, before I'd leaned out.

So, summoning up all my strength and willpower I grabbed the rope with both hands and hung on as tightly as I could.

It worked, I slowed my descent down to less than 5 mph by the time I collided with the jagged rocks at the foot of the abseil. It was still enough of a thump to wind me, and the rocks would have cut my head open if I hadn't absentmindedly put my wooly hat on. Why did I wear that on such a sunny day? No idea, but I'm glad I did.

When everything had stopped, I just lay there for a few minutes, getting my breath back, and contemplating what could have been when the pain from the main injury hit me. I'd given myself quite serious rope burns on both forearms and the pads of both hands as I'd applied the brakes. I was in agony, but I was glad I did it. Even though the pain was severe, I just laid there and smiled. I promised myself that I would never climb, OR abseil, without my safety buddies again !

*   *   *

One of the other life changing things that the Duke of Edinburgh's Award indirectly introduced me to, was hitch-hiking.

None of our group was old enough to drive, so if we couldn't get to our rock climbing sites by scrounging lifts off family or friends, there was only three options:

(1) Walk there - but the nearest place was 12 miles away
(2) Jump on a bus – unreliable on Sundays, also takes ages going through every minor village en route – and costly for three schoolkids with hardly any cash.

Or

(3) Hitch Hike.

So hitch hiking it was.

Nowadays, hitch – hiking is frowned upon as too risky and dangerous, but I think, like many other things in life, there is no more danger now, than there was years ago – probably less.

Years ago, many more crimes went unpublicised and undetected – but now, when even the slightest offence occurs it hits the local papers or national news bulletins.

I am glad, that when I was a teenager, the same fears didn't exist, as they would have deprived me of a very life enriching and rewarding experience.

As a schoolboy (I started hitch-hiking when I was 14) and later as a student, I hitched around the whole of England (probably the equivalent of 5 or 6 times) and the Channel Isles – my biggest regret is that I didn't have enough confidence in my linguistic skills to try it abroad.

Now that I'm a little more affluent than I was in those days, I am a car owner myself, but I always offer lifts to hitch-hikers. I consider that it's payback time for all the wonderful lifts that I received. Unfortunately, hitching has gone so much out of favour, that it is extremely rare to even see a hitch-hiker to pick up, on the road anymore.

Of course, like in any part of life, if you are adventurous, it can lead to some awkward situations (as you've already read) but this doesn't mean that you should hide yourself away, and get all your adventures second-hand from the TV or computer screens. Push yourself, and you will lead a far more rewarding life as a result.

In the next chapter I am going to tell of some of the scrapes that I got into whilst hitch-hiking. Please put them into perspective. For every awkward situation that I got into, I received at least fifty wonderful trouble free lifts.

Chapter 4

Hitch-Hiking & other stories

I started hitch-hiking when I was fourteen, and at that age didn't experience any problems whatsoever, but I was only hitch-hiking locally. The only off putting experience that we encountered at that time, was not knowing the technique – YES, there is a technique to hitch-hiking!

First of all, when we were going rock climbing we tried thumbing lifts all together and did get one or two after hours of waiting – but we were offered lifts much quicker if we split up and went on our own. Drivers don't like two or threes hitching together because it takes ages to get all of their bags on board and then everybody is cramped for the journey. Also, it meant that somebody had to sit on the back seat, and cautious drivers don't like anybody behind them.

Secondly, don't try to be helpful by walking down the road with your thumb out as, generally, drivers won't stop. They want to see what you look like, if you are tidy & presentable you'll get the lift, scruffy and evil looking – No.

So stand still, facing the traffic; and the best places to stand are at the top of a slip road to a motorway (illegal to go further anyway), or just after a roundabout, as the cars have slowed down for this, and so are more likely to stop, or at a layby.

One of the best lifts that I ever got, and *the* most memorable, was from a sliproad leading onto the A1(M) near Doncaster.

It was the schools summer holidays, and I was hitching down to Weymouth to catch a ferry to Guernsey in the Channel Isles. The sliproad was packed – it seemed like every northern student was travelling south on the same day. I had to wait my turn at the back of the queue. It took an eternity to reach the front – I reckoned that on a normal day, a half hour wait was a long time, but this day it took 3 hours just to make it to the front of the queue. Then, things got no better, I stood with my thumb out for a further hour. Everything was flying past, Minis, VW's, Transits. My arm was aching, I was fed up, I was seriously considering giving up and getting a bus into Doncaster then catching a train out.

Suddenly a car stopped – but not just any car, a beautiful gleaming old Bentley, leather seats, walnut dashboard, the lot.

I gasped as the window opened, "Any chance of a lift to London, mate?" I asked.

"Well, I'm not going into London, but I can get you very close."

"Cheers, thanks."

As I opened the door, and was about to get in, he asked. "Does your mate want a lift as well?"

Well, as you know from the spiel above, I always hitch-hiked on my own, so I was surprised at the question, but as I turned to look, another face was peering over my shoulder. Our knight in shining armour simply said, "throw your gear on the back seat, son. I suppose you want London as well?"

"Yer, Ta." Was the only sentence that we got out of my new 'mate' for over an hour.

The very posh owner of the car told us that he lived in Richmond in Surrey, and that he avoided going through London like the plague, but he would drop us near a tube station so we could easily and cheaply get into the centre.

After about an hour travelling he said, that he was getting a bit tired and needed a break, did we fancy something to eat?

I replied that I'd packed some sandwiches with me and that I was OK.

He retorted, "Sandwiches – boring. Besides if you made them this morning they'll be crisp by now. I mean a real meal. Don't worry, I know what it is like to be a student. - I'm buying."

I felt embarrassed, so said, "Thanks very much, but they need eating anyhow."

My 'mate' quickly replied "Thanks very much, I'm starving!"

So, Mr Richmond turned to me and insisted, "There you are, you can't sit and watch us eat a proper meal while you eat stale sandwiches."

I didn't know what to say, I just smiled and nodded.

Over a lovely 'motorway' dinner of steak & kidney pie & all the trimmings, my 'mate' eventually opened up.

"Do you know London at all?" he asked our driver.

"Not really, I'm in and out all the time, so have a passing knowledge, but you sound like you need something more specific."

"I just wondered if you knew where I could get a job. I was thinking maybe of trying the Docks."

"Well," our friend replied, "there are jobs all over, but I don't know of any specifically. Your best bet is to try one of the numerous employment centres."

"I can't I haven't got me cards with me."

In those days – pre-computer databases – you didn't just tell an employer your National Insurance number but you had to give him your 'cards' with the number on them.

"Well in that case, you're going to find it very difficult"

"But, don't you know of any jobs I can get without cards – the Docks or somewhere?"

"Not really. Why didn't you think to bring your cards with you?"

The lad went silent, then sheepishly replied "Lost them"

He tucked in to more pie, then looked up and said, "Truth is, I'm on the run from Hull Borstal."

I nearly choked on a piece of steak, and in total shock, stared at him wide eyed.

Our driver didn't seem to be worried at all, he merely said "Well in that case it IS going to be awkward. You'll have to sort out a job and tell the employer that you've left your cards at home and that you'll get them sent down. That should buy enough time for you to get two or three weeks pay, but then you'll have to play it by ear after that. What were you inside for anyway ?"

"Burglary"

No further comment was made until we'd finished the meal and our driver asked if anyone wanted a desert.

Our Hull inmate merely shook his head, whereas I replied, "No thanks, that was great, but don't forget I still have sarnies to finish, and my Mum would go ballistic if she thought she'd wasted her time making them."

"OK, it's back to the car then!"

My jailbird friend never shut up all the way down – it was as if he had just got a huge weight off his shoulders with his admission, and now he wanted to make up for lost time. He told us that he never burgled private properties – he wouldn't do that – that was stealing from real people. He only burgled businesses – most of them were crooks themselves anyway. He was making quite a decent living from it, until he got caught. Now he just wanted to go straight.

I wasn't sure I believed him, but his interesting stories meant that the journey passed really quickly, and before we knew it the Bentley slowed to a stop outside of a tube station.

"There you are fellas, Central London is 3 or 4 miles that way, I've brought you in further than I intended, but at this time of night there's very little traffic. Good luck with your next lift"

I thanked him, and with my "Cheers" still ringing out, Mr. Richmond–man was gone.

"What are you going to do now?" Borstalboy asked me.

I just wanted to get away from him, but I couldn't tell him that. I certainly didn't want hauling in by the Cops as an accomplice to anything illegal that he might have planned. Maybe I was misjudging him. I might be alright, He might be serious about going straight.

We walked towards Central London as I replied. "I have a bed waiting for me in Fulham, but . . ."

"Do you think they'll have one for me?"

". . . but as it's getting late I'm not going to go there."

"It's not that late. Only just turned nine!"

"Yeah, but it's at my mate Johnny's aunties who I've never met, and by the time we get there it will be gone ten. Too late for a stranger to call."

"But if she's expecting you . . ."

"No, there's no way I'm going to call round at this time of night."

I had her phone number, and I'm sure if I had called she'd have told me to still call round, but there was no way I was going to make that call with Jimmy Jailbird still hanging around.

So, we headed off for Central London, but as we were walking, Jimmy kept veering off the pavement to look in shop windows. "So what are you gonna do then?"

"Dunno, probably sleep in a waiting room at the station or even the toilets."

They'll all be shutting soon for the night."

"Not the main line ones like Waterloo or Kings Cross." I said.

"Bloody Hell, look at this one. It hasn't got a burglar alarm OR decent locks on the doors. It's just begging to be robbed. I'm coming back for this one if I don't get a job!"

I quickened my pace to try to put some distance between us, but he merely jogged a little till he caught up. He was gabbling with excitement. "D'you know it might be better if I don't get a job. I could clean up round here"

"And end up back inside before you know it!"

His face changed – "You're not going to report me are you?"

"Certainly not, each man to his own, but I certainly don't want involving in your little schemes either. It's best not to tell me anything about them."

That seemed to pacify him, because he smiled again and said "Look there's a sign for Victoria Station, just one mile. We might be able to get a kip there"

I didn't like the regular 'we' in his conversation, but how was I going to shake him off.

We stepped inside Victoria, and it was heaving. My initial plan of getting a place on a bench or in the waiting room was a non- starter as they were already full to bursting.

"What we gonna do then?" my 'mate' asked.

"Dunno I need to think"

"Have you lads got a problem?" the friendly stranger in the pink shirt and pinstriped suit asked.

"Not really, we were hoping to get a seat, that's all. We've been travelling all day."

"Well, I've arranged to meet a friend here but I can't find him. If you spot a fellow looking lost, carrying a black briefcase and an umbrella, would you tell him I'm here, and looking for him, please."

"OK"

Just about everybody was carrying a black brief case & umbrella. Some even had the bowler hat accessory too, but nobody was looking lost.

"Are you going to sleep in the toilets?" Jimmy asked me.

"Nope, too busy, too noisy, I'll probably just move on."

"Where are we moving on to?"

I was getting sick of this, I was just about to say not 'we' when . . . Mr City Slicker came back. "Have you seen him ?" he enquired.

"No," we said in unison.

"Well, I'm not waiting here all night for him. I'm going to do one last lap of the Station, then I'm going."

"Why don't you phone Fulham, then if you've got no other plans." Jimmy said, "I'm sure if you tell her the circumstances.."

"Look there is no way that I'm going to impose . . ."

"That's it then," He was back, "I can't find him, and I don't suppose you've seen him"

"Nope"

"Well, he was supposed to stay at my house tonight, and now there's a spare bed. Where are you boys staying tonight? There's a spare bed if you want it.

I'm going to look once more, and then I'll be back. You can tell me then if you want it."

We both looked at each other and said "Dodgy"

But, then Jimmy said "I don't mind going. It's better than sleeping in a toilet, and if he tries it on I'll thump him. He's just a little squirt, I could sort him out with one hand tied behind my back."

"What if you get to his house and there's ten of them?"

"Then I'll punch the first one and run, besides if you're there too, I'm sure we can sort it out, you look like you can handle yourself."

"Hey, don't include me in on this. I don't know if it is worth risking."

"Of course it is. It'll be better than sleeping in a toilet here, and when we get there we can just pop our heads inside the door, and if we don't like the look of it can turn around and walk away."

I was thinking about what he'd said, when our pinstriped friend turned up again. "Well that's it, he's not here. Do you lads want a bed for the night?"

"Yes" Jimmy replied for both of us and then grabbed hold of my arm and dragged me along. I could have easily resisted, but the thought of a warm dry house, even sleeping on the floor would be better than Victoria Station toilets. So I went along with it – besides I could still pull out at any time.

Our new friend told us that it was just a couple of hundred yards to his car, but when we got there we were both shocked. It was an old minibus, with still the first two rows of sets in, but the rest taken out for storage space, *and* the outside was painted up, psychedelically in orange, sky blue, pink and black.

I made a note of his number plate, just in case we did encounter any trouble – but I was pretty certain the police wouldn't need it if I just described this van.

London Boy saw the shock on our faces and merely shrugged it off, "The lads did that. I didn't mention that I was the manager of a pop group, did I?"

He drove us to a basement flat in Kensington, and declared, "Here we are, Chez Moi"

We stepped inside, and I cautiously enquired, "Is your band out gigging tonight?"

"Yes"

"And are they coming back here after that?"

"No, they're somewhere up North, probably a cheap hotel somewhere for them."

So we stepped inside. It was beautifully decorated in an arty-farty, chintzy style, but the chesterfield sofa he directed me to sit down on had seen better days. The arms were well worn, and quite thread-bare at the ends.

"Would you lads, like a cuppa? I bet you're parched if you've been travelling all day."

We agreed and he went into the kitchen to brew up.

Jimmy leaned closer and whispered. "Nice house – there you are I told you not to worry. Nobody else here, were OK."

"Does anybody take sugar? Ken(sington-man) asked.

"A couple for me." I replied.

"Good then," he retorted as he handed me the sugar bowl, "we'll just drink this and then we'll have to turn in. I'm up early in the morning."

He then turned towards the kitchen and casually threw back the killer punch, "You two just have to decide who is sleeping in my friend's bed, and who is sleeping in my double bed."

We both looked at it each other with the expression that said *I knew it.*

Then Jimmy said to me, "Well I'm taking the single bed."

"No problem, I said, "you can have the single. I'm quite happy sleeping here on this sofa."

When Ken returned, I told him of our arrangement, to which he replied, "There is absolutely no way that I am having anyone sleeping on my Chesterfield. That will ruin it."!!??!!

"OK," I said, "I'll sleep on the floor."

"No way," Ken replied quite shirtily, "you've heard my offer."

"Alright, then," I retorted. "You can have the bed," I said to Jimmy. "I'm out of here. I'd rather sleep in the Station toilets! Where's my bag?"

As I got up and went towards the door, Ken panicked, after all this was 1967 and homosexuality was still illegal. He thought I was going to the Police.

"Oh, there's no need for that. I've just remembered the band aren't coming back tonight. You can have one of their beds."

He showed me to a little cupboard under the stairs, which had an undersized single bed jammed into it. "You can sleep there," he said.

I took my rucksack into the closet, pulled the light switch on and noticed all the photographs that were pasted on the walls and ceiling. They were of various orgies, straight and gay, that had been held in his apartment. Thankfully, I also noticed, there was a Yale lock on the door. So I locked this, and dropped the sneck so that it couldn't be opened from outside with a key. Then I dug out my Swiss Army knife from my bag and left it open next to my bed, with a torch just in case. Finally, I could turn out the light and slip away into a much needed sleep.

I'd only been asleep a few minutes when BANG! BANG! BANG!

"Come on get up!" Ken shouted,

I knew it – I knew there'd be a catch.

I picked my knife up as I pulled on the light switch and looked at my watch. It read 7 am. I'd slept seven hours!!!

"Come on get up!" Ken yelled again, "I'm gonna be late for work."

I quickly pulled my clothes on, picked my bag up, and was ushered out off the premises. The manager said a quick "Sorry I've got to dash. The nearest Tube Station is about five minutes that way. Bye," as he jumped into the van.

Jimmy turned to me and asked, "What are you doing then?"

"Well. I'm taking the tube as far south as I can, from the High Street, and then hitching on to Guernsey" I wasn't telling him that I was booked in that night at my Aunties in Portsmouth, in case he invited himself.

"What about you?"

Ken's given me directions to the docks so I'm walking there this morning. If I get a job, I'll see if I can pick up a B&B too, if not I'm back there again tonight."

"OK," I said, "Good luck" then I set off at a good pace, hoping he wasn't following.

I didn't ask how last night went for him! - *(but he **was** considering going back for more!!!)*

* * *

I took the Tube to Hatton Cross, near Heathrow, which my map showed me was on the Great South West Road, an almost direct route to my next bed in Portsmouth. The progress there was easy, four good lifts and I met Craggsy there, as arranged, at my Aunt Carries House in Landport.

We both appreciated a comfortable night's sleep and a "full English" before we set off for Weymouth.

As usual we set off separately to make getting lifts easier, and arrange to meet up at 5pm at the Weymouth Ferry terminal, where we would also meet up with our friend Roly, who was carrying the tent.

The hitch-hiking went great. I got to Weymouth with no incidents, but the second lift was memorable.

My first lift dropped me at a roundabout only about ten miles out of Portsmouth. As I stood there with my thumb out I noticed the sign on top of the approaching car read 'Taxi', so I rapidly dropped my hand - but too late. It slowed down, and stopped right in front of me. Apologetically, I opened the door and told the driver that I wasn't after a taxi; I was hitch-hiking.

"Hop in," the driver said, "I'm not charging. I could do with the company on the way back to Weymouth. - Where are you going?"

I was gob-smacked. Not only was I being offered a freebie from a taxi driver, but they were going directly to where I wanted to be, and thirdly, the driver was a woman - and quite a good looker too!

When I had recovered my composure I said "I can't believe this, 99.9% of my lifts are from men, but never taxi drivers offering a free lift. Most women are scared to pick up a bloke in case he tries it on. Aren't you worried?"

"Not at all," she replied. "I'm used to picking up men as part of my job. Besides, if anybody gets awkward, I'll just hit them with this." And she pulled out a truncheon from the side pocket.

"Bloody Hell, have you ever had to use it?"

"Once or twice – always with drunks. Normally the threat is enough"

Obviously, I behaved myself all the way into Weymouth.

"Ferry Terminal, did you say?" my driver asked as she stopped the taxi right at the spot where I was meeting Craggsy.

Only problem now was that I was three hours too early. So, I bought an ice cream, and explored the beach and cliffs.

When I got back, Craggsy was waiting. We talked about our adventures so far as we waited for Roly. After a while we glanced at our watches – he was late! We couldn't phone him – this was 1967 and mobile phones weren't in use, so we waited and waited and waited.

Eventually, as it was starting to become dusk, we talked about making alternative plans to sleeping the night on the campsite that we had booked.

I had noticed some old Second World Was pill boxes on top of the cliffs when I was killing time, so Craggsy said, "Great, let's go up there before it gets too dark to see what we are doing."

When we arrived there, the pill boxes weren't as inviting as they appeared from the outside. They had been used regularly as a toilet, but as the night fell we had no alternative. We found half an old newspaper, (the other half probably used as toilet paper) and used it to carpet the area we were going to accommodate, and, ignoring the smell, managed to drop off to sleep within five minutes.

"Wake up, GET UP!!!" the voice that belonged to the hand that was tugging on my right foot was yelling at me.

"Who the bloody hell are you?" I cursed back.

"Weymouth police, You are not allowed to sleep here. Get up and get out."

"How do we know that you're the police? You could be just two muggers after our money."

"Because *I said* we are the Police."

"Not good enough mate, I need to see some ID before we go anywhere."

The voice produced a warrant card and flashed it in front of my eyes.

"That could be anything you just shown me. Probably bought it at Woolies."

Now I'd upset him. He shoved it infront of my face with vemon and snapped "Satisfied?"

"OK, but what's the problem with sleeping here?"

"Because it's illegal"

"Didn't see any signs when I came up here this afternoon"

"Smart ass eh? Do we have to arrest you for vagrancy to shut you up?"

"Are your cells nice and warm?"

"Right, you don't take a hint do you? Have you any money on you?

'Cos if you don't I'm arresting you for vagrancy."

"How much do you need"

"Enough to pay for a night in a doss house."

"Got much more than that"

"Show me" he snapped.

I produced my bank book, but as he tried to take it, I gripped it really tightly so that he could read it by his torchlight without taking it off me. - *I still wasn't sure.*

"OK," he said, his attitude softening, "if you've got this much money, why are you sleeping rough on my cliffs?"

So, I told him the story, of Roly not turning up & the problem we'll have later today if we don't have a tent to camp in Guernsey with."

He said, "OK, but you still can't sleep here. If I catch you anywhere in Weymouth sleeping rough again, I'll arrest you and you'll miss the ferry to Guernsey."

So at 3 am in the morning, we started walking out of Weymouth. Just as it started to get light again we arrived at a beautifully entitled place called Puddletown Forest where we made ourselves a bivouac out of fallen branches and leaves. Our mattresses were two mounds of leaves which enabled a very comfortable, undisturbed sleep for four hours. Then we had breakfast and set off on the return journey to the Ferry terminal. As we arrived we spotted a very worried looking Roly who thought we'd already gone to Guernsey and left him behind.

So, now totally equipped we all took the ferry to St Peter Port and enjoyed a great, blisteringly hot, two week vacation.

Did everything go hitch free?

No, and you wouldn't expect that of James Masters either!

After just four days we had to buy a sewing kit, and try to make as good a repair job of the rear of the tent as three ham-fisted lads could - after it had been attacked by a wild animal that had escaped from Guernsey Zoo !!!

There were twenty other tents on that campsite and a Tasmanian Devil, on the lookout for food, went past them all to attack ours!

The repair job was reasonable – the tent was once again inhabitable – but Thank God it didn't rain once in the two weeks we were there!!!

Whilst there, I also learned how to use a washing machine! Mum had always done the wash at home – so there was no need to know. But now we had decided to use the laundrette in St Peter Port, twice while we were there and a final time just before going home so that we had clean clothes to travel in.

The lads regretted nominating me to go first, 'cos it meant us all hitch-hiking home in beautiful matching pink outfits.

Nobody had told me that you needed to separate the whites from the colours!

I won't tell you what the lads called me!!!

*   *   *

Now, it must be stressed that I had hundreds of lifts in the nine years that I hitched up and down Britain between age 14 and 23. The vast majority were trouble free. However if you put yourself in these situations, some mishaps have to be expected. The above incidents were, as they say in war games lingo, collateral damage. They came as no surprise.

What did surprise me however was the Ford Transit that reversed back down the road to give me a lift near Bedford.

I had been left stranded by my previous lift who wasn't going as far as the Reading, that I'd asked for. He was only going to a small village about ten miles north of Bedford.

"That's OK," I said, "Please can you drop me off at a roundabout or sliproad close to your turn?"

"OK," my knight in shining armour said, "jump in."

Unfortunately, we had a mix up in understanding, because although I was quite specific in my request, my friend declared "I turn off here" as we came to a country lane in the middle of nowhere. "Bedford is about ten miles down that road."

It was a 60 mile an hour country road that cars were belting along. I had no option but to do, what earlier I told readers not to, and that was to walk with my back to the traffic with my thumb out. I only hoped that it wasn't the full ten miles before I came across a suitable roundabout that I could successfully hitch from.

I'd been walking for approximately a mile and, I would guess, a hundred cars must have flown past me.

Mini's, Maxi's, VW's . . . when suddenly, to a cacophony of screetching brakes and almost exploding tyres, a Transit van, almost unnoticeable inside a billowing dust cloud, was reversing towards me.

Now, this was *very* unusual, as once a vehicle has past a hitcher it never reverses back to them, especially if it is going so fast that it has to jam on the brakes that hard. And, this prospective lift continued to get more weird.

I was so desperate to get away from the spot I was at, that I didn't stay outside the van and ask where he was heading, anywhere would do. I climbed aboard the Transit as the driver, in a dark brown voice, asked "Where are you heading?"
(cheers to Ray Davies for that description)

As I replied "London" I looked at the driver and thought what a deep voice she had for a lady. Then I noticed that even though she was heavily made up, a noticeable stubble was growing through on her chin and upper lip.

Poor Woman, I thought, *I bet she's embarrassed by it all*, so I tried not to stare. I looked down towards my feet - but as I did I noticed her legs. She was wearing a checked tweed skirt, which rode up a little due to her driving position. This allowed more of her well muscled legs to show through her light coloured tights, as well as the matted black hair underneath them.

As we sped down the dual carriageway, she chatted freely, obviously less concerned about her manly looks than I was. I gave her the benefit of doubt that she was just an unfortunate woman, but still I slid slowly across towards the door, and jammed my rucksack down between us.

We started to talk about my life as a student at teacher training college when – WEE WAH WEE WAH WEE WAH, a blue flashing light overtook us and the driver indicated for us to pull over.

The policeman from the passenger seat walked over to the driver's window and indicated for it to be rolled down.

"Going a bit fast there weren't you?"

"I thought I was within the speed limit."

"What is the speed limit on this road?"

"Seventy"

"You obviously weren't paying attention to the signs, it is 50 along this stretch. Have you got your driving licence on you?"

My driver then fumbled for a few moments in a huge handbag, from which I'm sure I saw some taps protrude off a kitchen sink, and he eventually produced a licence."

"John Paul Williamson, eh?" the police officer said without showing any signs of shock, "Would you like to accompany me to my car, Sir?"

As he marched my driver away, his colleague came around my side, and this time indicated for me to wind down the window.

"How long have you known him?" he asked

"About 15 minutes. Until you pulled us over, I didn't know he was a fella.

I'm hitch-hiking back to Reading. I'm at College there."

"Well, if you take my advice, I wouldn't hitch-hike much further with this one!"

"I won't."

Just as he turned to leave me, the driver's door burst open, and he/she was back.

"F*****g pigs. Haven't they got some real criminals to catch instead of wasting their time on petty things like this!"

I said nothing, I just let him rant.

As we pulled away, I said. "D'you know, as time is getting on, I'm not sure I'm going to make Reading before nightfall. I think I'd better go to my friend's house in Bedford instead, and start again in the morning. Can you drop me at the next roundabout into Bedford, please?"

"Hey, there's no need to get out just 'cos of that. Nothing's changed, you're in no danger."

"I'm sure, but I'd still like to go to Bedford, please."

"OK, but there's no need"

I felt sorry for him, he obviously had problems, but I got out at the next roundabout just the same.

I did make Reading before it got dark!

*   *   *

As I've mentioned several times already, hitch hiking saves a lot of money and is good fun MOST of the time. The above anecdotes are about extreme things that have happened to me, and could have happened whatever mode of transport I was taking.

On some journey's, when my overdraft wasn't too unmanageable, I took the train into London from Reading, and a 'National' bus home. Most of the time the timetables of the two were compatible and I didn't have long to wait for the connection, but on one particular Christmas the connecting bus that I wanted was full, and I had to wait for the next available one four hours later. The bus station's little waiting room was jam-packed, and the benches outside were just too cold to sit on for long, so I had to find somewhere warm, where I could while away four hours inexpensively. I considered going for a meal, or sitting in a pub, but I couldn't make that last for four hours. So I decided to go to a cinema and watch a film through twice. It didn't really matter what I watched because I would probably fall asleep anyway!

I strolled back past Victoria Station to the main road where I asked around. I was directed to a couple of cinemas that were showing current blockbusters, but their prices were astronomical. So I changed my tactics. Next time I asked somebody for directions I told him that I wasn't interested in the film, just somewhere warm and cheap, where I could while away a few hours. It worked, I was directed to an old cinema, off the main road that was showing the classic film "Around the World in Eighty Days."

I sat down on the well worn, tatty seat about five rows from the back in this almost empty auditorium, and was just getting into the film when a man came and sat next to me, and after only a few minutes asked me if I'd like some popcorn.

"No thanks," I replied shirtily, "I'm trying to watch the film."

"I haven't seen you in here before." My new 'friend' said.

"No, that's 'cos I haven't been in here before." I replied keeping my eyes transfixed on the screen.

"Oh, whereabouts are you . . ."

I was sick of this, so I jumped up and said "I need the toilet."

I walked down the aisle and as I was halfway to the Gents I suddenly realised my mistake. I nervously glanced back, and sure enough he was following me. Then I gulped, 'cos when we were sitting down, I hadn't noticed his size – he was built like Arnold Schwartznegger! Normally, I reckon I could fight my way out of most situations, but if this one turned out awkward; - I was dead!!!

So, I speeded up my pace, got into the Gents well ahead of him and locked myself in a cubicle. I heard him come in, but I wasn't budging. I came to the cinema to while away some time, I wasn't too bothered if I spent most of it sitting in this warm toilet cubicle. I was determined to sit him out.

After about 15 minutes I heard the entrance door creak again – was it someone coming in? I didn't hear any more noise, it sounded like the room was empty. Or was it just a ploy?

I unsnecked the cubicle door silently, and opened it just slightly so that I could peer around. It seemed empty, so I opened the door fully and stepped out. It *was* empty! Quickly, I strode to the exit door, opened it and at almost a trot I made my way this time to the second row of totally empty seats. Still nervously glancing from the screen every few seconds to ensure that Arnie hadn't seen me and was moving in. After about ten minutes, I felt comfortable enough to settle down to watch the film properly.

My newfound relaxation lasted less than five minutes. A youngish man, dressed head to toe in black leather, decided that, of all the seats in this otherwise 90% empty cinema, he wanted to sit in the one next to me. He said nothing, just started to rub his leg up and down against mine.

THAT WAS IT, I was sick of all this. I jumped up and stormed out of the cinema. I still had about two hours to go before I needed to make my way back to Victoria Coach Station, but now I was spent up! With no money, only one thing for it – window shopping.

I wandered up and down the mainstreet looking at everything and nothing. I had by chance just started looking in a jewellers shop window when a voice behind me asked "Are you looking for anything in particular?"

Startled, I spun round – *Bloody Hell, it was Arnie!* Quick as a flash, I replied, "Yes, I'm looking for a ring for my girlfriend – we're getting engaged soon."

Undeterred, he moved closer, and said, "There are some nice one's here."

"Bloody Hell! Are those watches correct? Is that the time? I'm going to miss my bus."

I pushed passed him.

"Where are you going to?"

"Liverpool" I lied, as I ran off.

I didn't stop running until I entered the bus station, then after a few minutes to catch my breath, I went to the lockers, where I'd left my rucksack. I was just about to settle down onto a freezing cold bench, when Arnie came striding through the entrance. Like the Terminator, this guy just didn't give up! I put my rucksack up in front of my face and waited until he turned away to look at the other side's benches, then quickly slipped away into the toilets. Not a bad choice as it happened, even though I had to pay to go in, they were warm.

This time I didn't take any more risks. I stayed there, safely locked in my cubicle, until my watch told me that the bus to the North East was leaving in five minutes. I sped out of there, went straight to my stand, presented my ticket to the driver and climbed on board.

AT LAST, I breathed a huge sigh of relief – then in a fit of paranoia, I studied the occupant of every seat in detail;- surely my bodybuilding friend wasn't so desperate that he would be on board?

Satisfied, I chose an empty double seat towards the back and dumped my rucksack down on it so nobody could sit next to me. Another lesson learned!

That was the only time, of the numerous occasions that I took the bus that I had any problems. In periods of heavy usage – like Christmas and Easter I generally took the really early bus which was less crowded. Most people stayed in bed until a reasonable hour before escaping their slumber to travel. But not so Paul McCartney!

He apparently thought the same as me. Five O'clock in the morning – hardly anybody about. So in an obvious attempt to avoid the fans, there he was walking towards Victoria Station as I was walking away from the Tube to catch the early bus. He saw me and a look of dismay came across his face. I stared back at him for a moment, and thought that it might just be a look-a-like, -

but how many of them would have Linda and two kids walking with them?

"Morning" I said as I brushed past them.

Much relieved, I'm sure, he replied "Wotcha" and continued to walk hastily on his way.

Quite a change from my previous experiences! *(and I'm sure – his!)*

Chapter 5

Food Parcels to Reading

I was the first person in our extended family to go to College so a real fuss was made of me. Just like when I went to Grammar School, my mother went overboard in buying everything that was on the 'Essentials' list that had been provided.

When I left home my Mother cried; Dad was just glad to get rid of me.

I limped down Laycock Street, almost buckling at the knees, with an enormous rucksack on my back and a suitcase that was twice the size of the backpack. (no wheels on suitcases in those days). I could hear the glockenspiel (that I only played once) tinkling as it was hit by the course books (that I never opened).

My destination: Bulmershe College, Reading. This was day one of my training to be a PE teacher. If I could get to College carrying all this weight, I had already passed the physical!!!

Now, as I explained at length in the previous book, I never wanted to be a teacher, but I did quite like the idea of spending three years of playing rugby (and other sports) at the taxpayer's expense. I knew that there would be some other work involved, but I wasn't really interested in that. So, if I could just do the bare minimum to get through – that was my plan. Being kicked off the course or failing my exams was not an option, however, as my Mum (and Aunties) had sacrificed too much to get me there, and I was determined not to let them down.

Mum, too, was determined not to be forgotten; she sent me a letter about every three days when I first started Bulmershe, just to ensure that I was OK. These eventually dropped off to weekly then fortnightly then monthly. But, one day, early on and quite out of the blue, I found a note stuck to my Halls of Residence door:-

James Masters – 'Parcel at Porter's Lodge'.

Who, on earth, would send me a parcel to College?

All of the students on our 'PE corridor' saw the note too – they were probably more inquisitive than me, after all it was the first time that one of us had had a note pinned to their door.

"Who's it from Jimbo?" Pedro asked.

"Dunno."

"Aren't you interested?" Jono prompted

"Still be there tomorrow." I said, winding them up.

"You're not leaving it 'til tomorrow surely." Squalor retorted, with real pain in his voice.

"I might leave it all week, there's no hurry."

"But what if there's something in it that could go off" Benoit chipped in.

"Yeah, I suppose you're right." I said.

Then, without warning, I took off. I was the fastest runner of them all so, including the surprise element, I soon opened a 30 metre gap on the chasing pack.

It was like a Keystone Cops chase. I ran the 300 metres to Porter's Lodge and just had enough time to breathlessly ask the porter "Have you got a parcel for Masters?" before the beying pack piled through the door.

"Hostel and number" the stern assistant asked.

"Blackstone 30" I answered.

"Bloody Hell !" he retorted, as the door nearly flew off its hinges. "How many of you does it take to collect one parcel?"

"Sign here."

I duly did as requested then slowly walked outside.

"Looks heavy," Honey said, trying to get his hands on it.

"It is" I said, wrenching it from his grasp.

"Aren't you gonna open it now?" Rico implored.

"Yes, I am – *Back in my room."* I shouted back as I took off again, with the Keystone Cops in hot pursuit.

In my room, I quickly opened and then locked the door behind me, leaving the keys in the lock because Rico, my roommate also had a set.

They brayed, yelling and shouting, at the door for a good ten minutes. Then one bright spark (probably Rico) realised that I always slept with the window open.

Too late, I was one step ahead of them. I had locked it, but it was funny to see their pleading faces pushed up against the glass. Eventually to tease them, I went to the door, unlocked it, and left it wide open for them to enter.

The window theatre emptied and I heard the sound of their footsteps fade as they ran towards my room.

Of course, before they got there, I'd locked it again.

This time the hammering on the door was more intense, and the yelling and shouting had turned into death threats. In fear that they were going to smash it off its hinges, I eventually opened it – I had achieved what intended anyway!

The parcel's contents which included money, chocolate and clean underwear (which Mum knew I'd need by now) had all been stashed away in secret hiding places – the letter I put in my desk drawer, and all that remained was a fruit cake.

"What was in it then?" they all shouted in unison.

"Just a fruit cake and a letter"

"Just a fruit cake – is that all!!!"

"Well, you don't have to have any." I teased again. "More for me"

"Hey don't count me out," Squalor screamed, "it smells lovely.

"It is lovely, my Mum makes the best cakes in our whole family. The all get her to make one for Christmas. I'm gonna enjoy eating this." I replied making a fake gesture at putting it away into my wardrobe.

"You'd better be sharing that out soon" Benoit threatened, "or your life won't be worth living."

I pulled the parcel back, and declared "Well I ain't making the coffee as well!"

"OK, I'll make it," Squalor offered – but we all ignored him 'cos his cups would be as filthy as his room.

"OK, Benoit," I retaliated "It's your room for coffee, then"

Benny looked shell-shocked, but yelled out "Well you'd better bring your own mugs 'cos I ain't got enough for everybody."

So, the gannets descended on Benny's room and enjoyed an excellent cake, and a slightly less excellent cuppa.

And so a College tradition was started.

Everytime I received a parcel, the same Keystone Cops chase ensued and it always culminated in a cuppa in one of the lads rooms – a different one each time (except Squalor's).

Throughout my College career Mum sent me 5 more fruit cakes – even though I told her we had a perfectly good canteen at College, plus a College shop that sold mainly stationery, but also essentials like coffee, sugar, soap . . . (soap??? How did that get included as an essential???)

Also, I told her that the nearest village was only half a mile away, and there we could get everything we needed from the Spar. BUT she insisted - I think she thought that I lived somewhere near Timbuktu, and that I was lying about adequate food. She sent money too, because I think that she thought that I would spend all of my grant on beer. - *Silly!!!*

I settled into College life like this had been my true purpose in life. I was really glad that I was rejected by my first choice – Avery Hill – which was all marble and oak and stuffiness (or that is how it seemed at my failed interview).

In contrast, though, Bulmershe was modern and vibrant. I knew from interview that this was the College I wanted to be at. I wasn't sure, though, that they wanted me. Although my interview seemed to go well, I'd already been rejected by one college so my confidence was low. I yelled and jumped up and down with delight the day the letter came through to say I'd been accepted.

Not only did I now have to stand on my own two feet (almost – *I still took my washing & ironing home!*) but now I had to handle my own finances. Like most 'boarding' students I failed miserably at both. I only did my own washing when it was my turn to wash the team's rugby kit (about every 15 weeks – with visits home in between – *not bad for a student!*) but as for the finances . . . most of my money was spent behind the Students Union Bar . . . and I was forever going to see my bank manager to discuss my overdraft. Fortunately, he was quite good with me – understandable really as they made loads of money out of me in fees; so he played ball because I always paid the deficit off by getting a holiday job. This paid the arrears off before going back to College and back into the red the following term.

College also made me into more of a party animal than I used to be at home. Every Friday and Saturday there was either a live band on at College, or a disco, or a party at someone's house or Halls. No wonder I spent so much on booze!!!

The biggest surprise for me in all this partying was my first ever 'Formal'.

As a lad from the backstreets I'd never experienced this, let alone having to wear a bow-tie and tuxedo!

The other difficulty was finding a partner to take. I had recently split with my girlfriend, Mary, and I was in between. However, being at Bulmershe also helped in this department too, as we had only about a month earlier amalgamated with Easthampstead Park (an all girls' college) so this boosted our girl boy ratio from the very reasonable 4:1 up to the now fantastic five girls for every fella. Surely, even I couldn't fail to get a partner at these odds.

In the common room at Easthampstead, I had regularly chatted with two girls that I fancied, Mary, (*a different one*), who was good looking and very bohemian, training to be an Art Teacher, and Brenda, who was stunningly good looking, but way out of *my* league.

So, puffing out my chest, and plucking up all of the courage I could muster I turned to Mary and said, "It's the College Formal next month, Mary, if you're not going with anyone, I'd like to take you."

Cupid's arrow never hurt anyone as much as that day when he shot me down. Mary replied, "Sorry, I've already checked the date and I'm back at home that weekend with my FIANCE."

I nearly collapsed, all my strength had drained from me, as I squeakily turned to the goddess, Brenda, and pleaded, "Well looks like it's gonna have to be you, Brenda, how are you fixed?"

"I'd love to come," she replied, "I'll ring home and see if Mum can bring a long dress up."

I couldn't believe it, I really fancied Brenda in the first place, but I was so convinced that she'd turn me down without a second thought, I was too scared to ask.

I almost did a triple somersault in celebration, but still trying to keep up my cool exterior said "Good, that's settled then, we'd better discuss arrangements over a drink. Tomorrow night if that's OK. We'd better not go to the College Bar 'cos we'll never get anything done. How about Chequers in Woodley?"

"That sounds great to me," Brenda replied.

"Brilliant, I'll meet you at the front gate at 8pm then, if that's alright."

"Yes, that's fine."

"OK, got to go now – Sociology tutorial, see you tomorrow." I cooly walked out of the common room and as I turned the corner towards my lecture room I jumped sky high, whooping and punching the air. If I had been anywhere else the passing people would have thought I was mad, but here they all knew me as one of the PE students, so they didn't bat an eyelid!

The following day seemed to contain forty hours and every one dragged through slowly. Don't ask me what lectures I had that day 'cos I just daydreamed through every one. Eight o'clock finally arrived and I had been anxiously waiting at the gate for ten minutes already. At ten past eight I realised that it had all been too good to be true, and started to walk back to my room when this vision in light blue floated around the corner (fashionably late).

"Sorry I'm late, my room-mate lost her key and we had to search for it, otherwise I would have had to leave her mine."

"OK, but don't let it happen again," I joked, "Otherwise our dates off."

Who said there's going to be another one after tonight!" she smirked, comfortably putting me in my place.

We discussed the arrangements for the Formal about 28 nights over the next month. I'd never been so happy.

Eventually the big night came around, I looked like a very stiff penguin in my tux, and Brenda – Brenda looked like Brenda. I showed around the dance areas with her on my arm like an overproud peacock. Even Marty Dragon, one of the rugby team couldn't deflate me when he retorted "How does an ugly git like you manage to bring a gorgeous girl like that to the Formal?"

I put him down with, "Marty, if you don't know, you've got no chance of doing it yourself!"

We then walked into the Refectory where a superb buffet was set out and we listened for a few minutes to the Jamaican Steel Band that were playing. Then I said, shall we go into Bridges *(the main lecture theatre)* because the band are playing in ten minutes and I think it will be packed.

"Yes, alright, but I wish Marmalade were still playing."

"I know, but apparently they asked for a grand more money after their record had gone to number one in the charts, so we gave them the boot. Blue Mink are a pretty good alternative though, they've already had a number three in the charts with Melting Pot"

Quite impressed with my knowledge (that I'd only just looked up) Brenda said, "Oh, I didn't know that was them. I like that one."

*   *   *

Brenda was my girlfriend for the rest of my first year, I even went to stay at her house in Malvern during our summer holidays. I was on cloud nine, my mother was delighted too when I told her that I was looking for a ring to get engaged.

But, when we returned to College after the summer break, I'd had plenty of time to re-think and I'd decided that 19 was far too young to be planning my future – especially when the new term also brought a new intake of dozens of young girls that were desperate for an older boyfriend.

So, we split. I'd always intended asking Brenda to go out with me again later in my College life but every time I was without a girlfriend she always seemed to have a boyfriend and vice versa. So I moved on - to Annie – more about that later.

Brenda and Jan, ran our Rugby Team Supporters Club between them so I saw her everytime I played, but unfortunately I didn't make the first team too often that year. I didn't like the captain, (the feelings, I know, were mutual), I thought he was the worst and dirtiest captain that I'd ever played under. But when he deliberately injured one of our best players, Dai Thomas a Welsh Schools International, in a training session, I'd had enough.

I had been talking to a PE teacher on a school visit that was part of my course, when I mentioned that I was disgruntled with the College team and he told me that he played for Redingensians Rugby Club, and why didn't I come along that weekend - he was sure I'd get a game.

This was one of the best things that ever happened to me, because I borrowed a bike, and cycled out to the place that he'd described to me, but I couldn't find the Club. I cycled round and round the area, but as it was getting close to kick off time decided to go back to College. As I was cycling along, I noticed some rugby posts in the distance so hurriedly sped towards them hoping not to miss kick off.

I met a man at the gate who was directing in traffic and spectators, and asked, "I'm looking for a game, are you short in any of your teams?"

"I think the Fourth Team only have 14 men, if you hurry up you might just catch them before they go out to warm up."

I dashed into the changing rooms, the Fourth Team Captain was delighted to restore his team to the full compliment. "Whereabouts do you play?"

"Anywhere in the backs, but I prefer full back."

He threw me a green & white hooped shirt without a number on it, and said, "Full back it is then, see you on the pitch." And he was gone.

It was only when the shirt hit me that I realised – Redingensians play in all black – who had I just joined?

I put the shirt on jogged out of the changing rooms, and looked around for clues. The sign above the Clubhouse proudly proclaimed 'Reading RFC founded 1898'

I had accidently landed a game with one of the best clubs in the County.

I scored two tries that day – God knows who the opposition were, and the next week I was promoted to the Third Team. I can't remember if I scored in that match but I do know it was away at Basingstoke, because I achieved a good write up in the local paper, and once again I was promoted; to the Second Team. I played two games for them before, on one of our training nights, I was practicing my kicking when the First Team Captain, Brian Dilley, and Fly Half , Ian Honnor, walked over to me.

"Hi," Brian said as he introduced himself, "how are you doing?"

"OK," I replied, trying to second guess what's coming next.

"You've been doing alright since you joined the Club. I've been hearing rave reports from the Second Team about your performances at full back, but it's a fly half that we're short of in the first team. How do you feel about giving it a shot in that position?"

"Great," I said, I played County Schools' fly half last season, before I came to College."

"You did? - Well, why are you playing full back in the Seconds?"

"Because I never play fly half for a new team until I see what their pack and scrum half are like. A bloke can spend a lot of time in hospital if you haven't got those in place."

Brian seemed delighted, and told me, "Well you'll have no problems in those departments here, we have a superb pack, and Ted Goodhew is the County scrum half."

"Were playing Aylesbury on Saturday and Ian here is injured. It's your shirt if you want it"

"OK," I said delighted, "What time does the bus leave?"

I didn't sleep on the Friday night before the game, but I wasn't worried; this was usual for me the night before a big game, and this was a BIG game. Aylesbury hadn't been beaten at home for eighteen months!

During the game the two sets of forwards went at each other, hammer and tongs. Neither pack was totally dominant, but no quarter was given. It was brutal.

When we won the ball I quickly passed it out so that our backs could have a good go at the opposition, but the Aylesbury tackling was superb. When they got the ball they couldn't break down our defence either. It was a stalemate. Until with only five minutes left I decided it was time for action. It was our put in to the scrum just ten metres from their line. I signalled to Ted that I was dropping back further than usual. He knew what that meant – I was lining up for a drop goal – unfortunately the opposition flankers knew that too. Our hooker won the ball cleanly, it was swiftly channelled back to our number eight's feet, Ted took the ball from between them and threw a pass back to me with perfect speed and pinpoint accuracy. With the opposition flankers bearing down on me I struck the worst drop kick that I have ever done in my whole rugby career. I hit the top of the ball, it stayed low, it bobbled, it skewed but it just scraped over the bar by millimetres. We won the game 3-0.

Aylesbury were defeated at home for the first time in a year and a half, and I became an instant hero. All the players and supporters wanted to buy me a drink, but I was still cheesed off with the manner that I'd executed the kick.

Needless to say, I was still in the team for the next game against R.M.A. Sandhurst. They caused us problems for the first thirty minutes but after that we took control. I scored a drop goal and penalty in that game and so again retained my place.

We. as a club, hadn't been beaten for quite a while now, so the next game came as quite a shock, but also probably did us a lot of good. It was against Old Emanuel in the City. They had a fly half, Dodds, who had a kick like a mule on him.

Our pack tried hard to gain territorial advantage, but everytime we got into their 22, he kicked us back 60 metres down the field. Our team folded and they beat us by 30 points!

I didn't play particularly well, but then again nobody did. In my case though, as the 'new boy,' my selection was hanging in the balance. So, I was very relieved when I was again picked for the next game. But, then, shock of horrors, I realised that it was College holidays – everybody *had* to go home as there was a course being run on the campus so I'd already booked my ticket on 'The Highwayman,' a new rail service to the North East that was then being trialled by British Rail. So, I had to break the news to the Captain.

At my last training session on the Thursday evening before going home, he came over to me and asked if I would be willing to travel back to College early if they paid my travel expenses, and provided accommodation for the night.

They were desperate – I was delighted.

The game was the semi-final of the County Cup, held on the neutral ground of Bracknell, against the mighty Windsor.

The second class rail fare from Middlesbrough that they offered me was £30, which at today's rate would be over three hundred pounds – a fortune to a cash strapped student – so I happily accepted their deal, and then hitch-hiked down in order to pocket the cash!

It was a very windy Saturday on the afternoon of the Semi. Reading won the toss, and decided to play against the wind in the first half.

Windsor threw everything at us but our defence held firm, so we turned around

0-0 at half time. Now it was Reading's turn to exert all of the pressure with the almost gale force wind behind them, but still they couldn't break down Windsor's resolute defence.

With just 15 minutes to go, Reading won a line out on the left closer to the ten metre line than the 22 – just the position I favoured when I practiced my drop kicking, but a bit further out than I liked. Including the angle it was just over forty metres – but I had a gale force wind helping me. So, bearing in mind that fortune favours the brave, I set myself up.

Before he passed me the ball Ted, later told me, he knew exactly what I was going to do.

The ball, as usual, arrived perfectly from my scrum half. The opposition flankers weren't pressuring me because they didn't expect a drop kick from so far out. I just concentrated on keeping my eye on the ball, head down and striking it perfectly – the wind would do the rest. It went like a dream, literally, I lifted my head when the ball was about 15 metres off my boot, and then turned and trotted back to the halfway line, I knew it was over. The crowd went hysterical, the newspaper headline read

"Deputy Masters puts Reading in Rugby Final"

I'd had newspaper write ups before, but this was my first ever headline (I still have it in an album to this day)

That wasn't the end however, there was still fifteen minutes of the match to go, and we all expected Windsor to come raging back. We were wrong, however, because the dropped goal seemed to have knocked the stuffing out of them. Reading camped inside their 22 for the rest of the match, but couldn't find a way over their line. With approximately 3 minutes left we were awarded a penalty inside their 22 but way out on the right hand touchline. Brian threw me the ball and asked "Do you think you can do it?"

"I'll have a bash," I replied.

It was at a tricky angle, but made worse by kicking back into now a cross wind. The only way that I was going to get it was by using the elements to my advantage.

I aimed the ball about 15 metres beyond the left hand post and hoped the wind would do it's job.

Just as I was about to start my run up, a big booming, drunken voice yelled, "He's gonna miss that by a mile, it's not even pointing at the posts!"

It made me abort my run up and rethink my assessment. I looked at the ball, then the posts, then the ball again. I imagined its flight in my head – it still seemed correct, so I hit it. The ball as expected flew high, way past the posts but then almost stopped dead as the wind caught it. It took hold of it and curled it to the right – smack between the posts. The crowd went crazy, I just turned in the general direction of the heckler and snapped "Empty vessels sound loudest," before jogging back to half way.

Reading 6 – Windsor 0.

We were in the Cup Final, and I'd just hit the two best kicks of my whole career in one match, and on top of that, I'd paid back a substantial amount of my overdraft.

The Final against Marlow was a bit of a let down; no team really shone, but Reading eventually ground them down to win 16-6. I only scored two conversions, but this time it was the partying afterwards, not the match, that was memorable.

The first ever, brand new and shiny County Cup was presented to Reading, and we went upstairs in the clubhouse at Maidenhead to celebrate. Somebody filled the cup with champagne and passed it around the bar. I duly took my drink, but, even though I don't like champagne, this was the worst I'd tasted, - SILVER POLISH! Some idiot had forgotten to wash it clean of the silver polish before pouring the champagne in!

That night I didn't put my hand in my pocket, as all of our friends and supporters were buying drinks for us.

Then, somebody suggested going out for a celebratory meal, to the local Indian. I'd never been for an Indian meal before, so forever the adventurer, I agreed, but thought I'd better go to the loo first or I'd not make it into Reading.

The toilets were downstairs, near the changing rooms so off I went while the other players were collecting their gear.

I came out of the changing rooms to a cacophony of yelling and screaming.

"Stop him, STOP HIM." The beying pack was yelling as they were chasing someone down the stairs. Needing no further prompting, I joined them, and flattened him in a tackle that was better than any I'd made in the 'Final'.

He stood up and punched me in the mouth.

I didn't feel a thing 'cos I was so drunk, "You stupid b*****d," he said, "You stupid b*****d, that was just a joke." The mangled County Cup was then produced from under his body, and it wasn't new and shiny anymore. Fortunately for him, (and me), the Club paid for its repair.

So a little worse for wear, we all piled into the 'designated driver's' cars and headed for the 'Taj Mahal' in Reading. The owners were a little startled at so many people turning up unannounced (maybe we should have phoned first), but were only too happy to put four tables together to make the grand banquet that we ordered. I hadn't a clue what I was eating because, as a novice, I left it up to Mikey to order for me.

The papadums came, and we all piled into them, as if we hadn't eaten for a week. Paddy (our open-side psychopath) was dry after eating more than his quota, so yelled for the carafe of water to be passed down the banqetting table. The lads at the far end retorted that it was needed and, in less polite tones, for him to get his own. Paddy wasn't having this. He stood up on the table and walked down the centre to get his water. On the way after scattering most other objects out of the way, he tripped over a flower vase, and flew head-first towards the window. Fortunately, the velvet curtains saved him, and as he grabbed them, the pelmet, curtain rail, and half the wall plaster came crashing down. Amidst the plaster dust and splintering wood, Paddy's right foot managed to knock one of the candles over and set fire to the serviettes. Fireman Paddy quickly regained his composure and whilst shouting "Fire, Fire" threw the remaining contents of his jug over the flames, but mainly over anyone sitting behind them. The lads on the far side retaliated by grabbing jugs of water off the adjacent empty (they were now) tables, and so the (fun) fight started. The management and waiters all flew out of the kitchen to quell the uprising. The boys sat down after a stern warning.

I made for the door.

It was all too much for me, I think it was the smell of the Indian food, or it may have been the silver polish, (it can't possibly have been the amount of beer that I'd had to drink), - but I was ill. Fortunately, I managed to make the gutter outside of the restaurant, before I staggered back to the steps leading up to the entrance and sat there with my head in my hands. It must have only been about ten or fifteen minutes, before the door behind me crashed open and the Team, led by Paddy, came bursting past me. "Come on, Come on" they yelled, as they ran off down the road, with the kitchen staff, equipped with carving knives in hot pursuit.

I was in no state to run, I was taken prisoner and held hostage until the damages and food were paid for. Sheepishly, one of the committee members came back to release me with a wad of notes that he'd collected from the lads and he signed for the damages to be met by Reading Rugby Club.

Although, the Club won't have been happy with the two bills that they were presented with from that momentous day – I'm sure they wouldn't have changed anything if it meant missing out on being the first name on the new *(soon to be repaired)* County Cup.

That was the last time, I saw most of those guys, as the following season I was back playing for College, but I'll always have fond memories of playing for that Club, especially the meteoric promotion through the teams to eventually play only a memorable FIVE games for the First Team, culminating in a Cup Final!

Chapter 6

Top That

Well; I couldn't top that; but life at College still went on outside of rugby.

The focus of our first year at College was Primary Education. We went out on numerous 'observation visits' to see how different schools were organised, and how their teachers fitted into their systems. We also watched individual teacher's teaching styles to gain a greater insight into how we were going to try to perform ourselves on our fast approaching FIRST teaching practice.

Although I had enrolled as a trainee secondary school teacher, my first TP was to be in a primary school (very sensible, as at 19 I may have only been one or two years older than some of the secondary pupils I would eventually teach!)

The only downside, *that I could see at that time*, was that I was expected to teach every subject from Music *(that's where the glockenspiel comes in),* Geography, Arts & Crafts, English, Maths, History, etc.

So obviously, I had tuition in all of these, and more, subjects before going out on TP; but I was still unsure if I was prepared enough to teach some of my less proficient subjects. Fortunately, though, I was only going to be teaching them to seven year olds – how hard could that be?

The first year PE students all gathered around our main noticeboard on the day of announcement, desperately praying that they hadn't been sent to one of the 'rough' schools. I wasn't as concerned as most, because none of the schools that the College used were that rough – not compared to the primary school that *I* had been educated in.

I looked down the list, found my name, and was elated to find that I had been given a school in Caversham, one of the poshest parts of the Reading area.

I was to start there at 8.45am the following Monday – *coach number four from outside the lecture theatre.*

The students on my bus were all going to the North & West of Reading, Tilehurst, Pangbourne, Caversham, etc., and they piled on the bus nervously chattering about their expectations for the day. Unusually for me, I was quiet.

Squalor, who was at Pangbourne, noticed. "You OK, Jimbo?"

"Yeah, I'm just pooping myself a bit. I don't mind teaching the kids, but I'm kicking off with a short staff meeting where I'm being introduced to the Staff. Don't fancy that at all."

"Oh, unlucky, I just have to meet the form tutor, who will take me from there. Don't fancy yours."

"Cheers, mate. I feel a lot better now."

The journey was only 20 minutes and I was one of the first off. I was glad I didn't have to wait until last.

In the staff meeting, I could read the expressions on all of the nine staff's faces. The older ones were looking at me thinking *he doesn't look old enough to get served in a bar.* (They were right, I had a baby face and I was 23 years old before every pub would accept me!!!). The younger ones were thinking, *poor bairn I remember myself exactly what it was like.*

I was greeted by everybody and in reality, it wasn't as scary a meeting as I imagined. The Headmistress personally introduced me to Roger, as it was his class that I was going to share.

Roger took me to one side and told me the set up, what they were covering that day and asked me just to observe how everything ran on the first day. Then we braved the kids. Roger introduced me to them: "This is Mr. Masters, he is a student from Bulmershe College, and he will be helping me to teach you for the next four weeks."

The class gave a half sigh/half cheer. I looked around at all their happy smiling faces, they were all little angels; I knew that I was going to have no trouble from them for the next four weeks.

They say that first impressions can be false – a book and its cover, etc. – but that was a fairly accurate assessment of the group. I loved working with them. The vast majority of them *were* little angels, - but *SO-O* tiring.

After each day of that TP, I was going back to College, having dinner, preparing the next day's lessons and going to bed. I think that the latest I went to bed throughout that period was 8.30 pm!

Eventually, of course, I became a secondary school teacher and things became easier, but if I had gone into Primary I would definitely NOT have lasted the twenty years that I did in Secondary.

(Good) Primary School teachers deserve double their salary!!!

One amusing little incident that happened approximately three months after I had finished the teaching practice was that I received a letter from a lovely little girl from my class, called Stella Rotczyk. However, before I eventually received it, it had gone to Berkshire College of Agriculture, then Easthampsted Park College, and was eventually delivered to my home address in Middlesbrough!!!

(Ah! The GPO as it used to be!)

She asked me if I liked the chair *(choir)* singing, and wasn't that a terrible storm the other night and it was on the hottest day of the year!!!

Dear Stella, (who will be in her fifties now)

Thanks for the letter – It got to me eventually – sorry I didn't reply.

*   *   *

The most enjoyable, and most interesting part of my College course came at the end of my first year – The Wye Trip.

We had been building up to this for months, but now as the summer term was rapidly approaching it was imminent.

The Wye Trip was to be a canoe expedition, in a group of at least four, over seven days, paddling down one hundred miles of the River Wye. This might sound severe, but in fact was a jaunt for most of us as the river flowed so fast in the upper reaches that it was easy to cover more than twenty miles a day, but in the lower reaches where it was slow and tidal, - progress was sluggish.

The first year PE students were encouraged to make (under supervision) and name their own fibreglass canoes, so there were many variations of "Wye Bother" and "Wye Do It" in our flotilla.

As you have learned from previous chapters, outside of my various sports, I had precious little time to do anything else; building a canoe would mean missing more lectures or handing in even less essays. So sensibly, (for me, I thought), I would just use one of the Colleges stock of old canvas canoes – BIG MISTAKE.

Once canoes had been made, *or borrowed*, it was time to test them (and us) out.

Our first session was at an indoor pool where we learnt the basic paddling strokes and how to get out of a canoe if it capsized.

Then it was out onto moving water - much more difficult because, although the current helped to move the boat along in one direction, when you went the other way it was arduous. Also as you swung the canoe around to change direction, the current had a habit of flipping the boat over and put you underneath it.

I didn't realise how muddy and horrible tasting the River Thames was, at Pangbourne, until I'd experienced it for myself.

Fortunately, as any well organised group should be, we picked out several of the stronger students who were to be the back markers on the trip. They were highly trained in First Aid, and rescue procedures, as well as being the strongest paddlers. Whilst we were practising, two of them stood on the bank, keeping an eagle eye out for anybody in difficulty, whilst two were in the water in their canoes, ready to spring into action as soon as the call came that there was somebody that needed help.

So when I capsized my canoe making a turn, just near the bridge, I knew that I simply needed to go through the drill that we had been trained to do at the swimming baths.

Easier said than done!!!

My first reaction on flipping over was to panic and take a mouthful of muddy, horrible tasting Thames water, then, to try to clamber out of the cockpit anyway I could. After what seemed like half an hour (but in reality only seconds) I re-gathered my composure and went through the Drill; both hands on the underside of the canoe (which of course was now uppermost) and banging loudly to attract attention, showing that I needed help. At this point the rescue boats should arrive and put the nose of one canoe into one of my hands, enabling me to lever myself up on this and . . . continue happily paddling away.

So, I waited, --- and then banged again. --- I WAITED AND BANGED AGAIN, but now rapidly running out of oxygen decided that it was time to do something myself. I had to get out, so tried to push out of the cockpit – but I was stuck. I tried again – no success – so, in a REAL panic now I started tearing at the edge of the spraydeck to release it manually. Fortunately, it came off quite easily!!! Two sculls sideways with my arms and I was out, back on the surface frantically gulping down fresh Berkshire air.

I glanced across to see how close my rescuers had got, and they were all still there, on the bank, holding their sides in hysterical laughter.

Thanks lads – I could have died – but that probably would have been even funnier!!!

SO, now I was totally prepared to take on the mighty River Wye.

Well, not quite yet.

We still had to sort out our Campcraft and packing.

(The River Wye, by the way, is classed as one of the easiest rivers [if not THE easiest] to paddle on – except for one point --- SYMONDS YAT!!!).

The tents, cooking equipment, etc., were issued to each group and we all went outside onto the rugby pitches to erect the tents and check the other gear out.

The following week, we had to put everything to practical use; on our three day rock climbing course in the Peak District, Derbyshire.

We all arrived at our site, erected our tents and set about cooking our first, of many, meals under canvas.

As my group sat on some fallen rocks huddled around our small camping gaz stoves, there was a huge explosion to our right, and a human fireball came flying out of what was left of one of the tents.

It was Rico, he had decided (against instruction) to assemble and test his stove *inside* the tent.

We all jumped up, grabbed hold of him, and rolled him over and over on the damp grass, until the flames were extinguished.

Apart from being a bit singed, he was uninjured, but in a state of shock, all he could say was, "Look at me jacket, look at me jacket. I only bought it last week for this trip."

Lucky boy, he'd decided to check his stove inside, because the weather was so damp and cold outside. (Bloody soft, Southerner !!!)

*   *   *

And so to the River Wye.
We were now all totally prepared.
(Ha, ha, ha!!!)
We travelled there in minibuses, with the canoe trailers weaving along behind them, and our lecturers sharing the emergency rescue Land Rover behind these.

Our launching point was Glasbury – high up in the peaks. The water was shallow but fast. We had only paddled about 200 metres before we hit our first rapids – literally.

It wasn't a big rapid but it was our first and some of the group panicked. One of the canoes hit a rock, right on the nose. The current got hold of it and swung it round, jamming its tail against another rock. Our rescue team watched in horror as two of the girls in a big double kayak came thundering along, weren't able to change direction, and hit the stranded canoe broadside. The single kayak split into two halves and it's occupant was momentarily carried along on the nose of the double, before he fell off.

It was Rico, our human fireball from the Peak District!!!

And I thought I was a disaster magnet!

Fortunately, one of the minibuses was still unloading some of the equipment before going back to College. So Rico took a lift from them, back to College, to return two days later – with a new canoe – further down the route.

Needless to say, nobody wanted to paddle anywhere near him for the rest of the week.

The last ones into the water was of course our safety group, we'd packed everything into our canoes as instructed at College, except for one minor detail – the empty plastic litre bottles that we were supposed to carry for extra buoyancy were all full of Shed's homebrew – if one of US capsized the kayak would sink like a stone.

We were working on the theory that the bottles wouldn't be full for long, and they would be once again bouyancy aids within a few days!

One problem this initial lack of buoyancy created was that our Kayaks' sat pretty low in the water, and as the water was very shallow anyway, we scraped along the bottom in various places. That was fine for the rest of the group who had built their own fibreglass canoes, but for me it meant that if I contacted one sharp rock the canvas would slit very easily.

I had only paddled about fifty metres when I heard that jagged rock do its job.

The canoe immediately filled with water, and I abandoned ship.

I walked the stricken vessel back to shore, dragging it up the bank behind me. On the grass I dug out my emergency repair kit, sewed the tear back together and then covered the lot with duct tape. This lasted for all of five minutes before the outside tape floated off and the rest of the repair started to let water in again. Fortunately, though, I was still able to proceed as it had slowed the flow considerably. It was letting in about five millilitres of water for every stoke I made – so 100 strokes = half a litre of water splashing about inside my canoe. I called the group to an emergency stop about every three miles to empty my canoe, as I was in danger of disappearing.

I travelled the full length of the Wye, constantly wet around the legs, but worse still, when we made camp each night I had to hang out all of my clothes, and sleep in a wet sleeping bag every night. So much for the double bagging, and double knotting system – which didn't work!

I was fortunate once again, in that the weather was kind, and the warm sunny conditions meant that the clothes were pretty dry if we were going out in the evening – (but then were pretty wet again the next day!!!)

Our second night's camp was at a designated site. (Other nights we could camp where *we* had arranged – so *our* sites were generally very close to a pub!)

The PE lecturers had booked us all in on Farmer Brown's land just down from

Hay-on-Wye, so that they could check that everybody was faring OK. Best of all, though, they had organised a dinner of chicken and chips for everyone at the George Hotel. This lunch stop was very well received! We played bowls there (the old fashioned nine pin type) and also had a couple?!? of drinks. When everybody got up to go, being the safety group, we had to go last, so we stayed for another beer before setting out to paddle the easy couple of miles to Farmer Brown's.

I've never known the conditions change so much in just a couple of hours! The wind was howling, making it difficult to walk straight, and when I got into my canoe I had to constantly slap the water with my paddle to stay upright! – At least I think it was the weather that was causing the problems!

Needless to say, we never drank that much on a lunchtime for the rest of the trip, because, on consideration, it might not have been the weather that was the problem!

That didn't mean we stayed teetotal for the rest of the trip – just that we limited ourselves to one pint at lunchtime, and made up for it in the evening!

After Hay, the next noteworthy stop we made was at another designated site on the river bank at Hereford. We were looking forward to this one, as the older lads at College had told us that it was just a short walk into town – and a great night out.

So I once again emptied the water from my canoe as I pulled it up on the bank, picked out my less dishevelled clothes and hung them out to dry before preparing an early evening meal. After the meal, all of the boys got ready in their dry gear as I pulled on my slightly damp clothes, and we hit the town.

We hadn't walked far, when we heard the sweet tones of "Chirpy Chirpy Cheep Cheep" coming from a nearby disco. So we made a beeline for it, and asked the doorman if it was alright for us to go in.

"Sure," he said looking a little nervous, "£1 each, but no trouble tonight lads, please."

Strange request we thought, but then looking at the eight of us, hot off the river (or in my case 'cold'), I suppose we could have looked a bit rough.

Inside the disco, we asked the barman for eight pints. - He couldn't move quickly enough to help us.

What a nice place I thought.

We later asked the DJ for a couple of requests and he too was exceptionally courteous and again said that he wanted no trouble, but he would get them on as soon as he could.

I looked around the group, and wondered what was it about us that suggested we might be trouble? OK, we were a bit dishevelled after roughing it in a tent and on the water for four days, but apart from not shaving for a few days our appearance was well kept, short, neat hair, most (apart from me), tall and muscular. Then the penny dropped:- "The SAS are based here in Hereford," I whispered to the lads. "They think WE are SAS!"

We played on it for the rest of the night. Everytime we went for a drink the crowd parted before us. If we went outside, the door was held open for us, etc.

I think we'll go back to Hereford again one day!!!

The next day's paddling, we knew, was going to be a long slog as we tried to get as near to Ross-on-Wye as we could, because we wanted to be fresh when we tackled SYMONDS YAT.

The plan worked very well; we made Ross just before lunchtime, stopped to eat (I emptied the canoe again) and then we pressed on; earlier than normal and totally sober to Symonds Yat.

We didn't need to look at our maps to see how far off S.Y. we were, as we could hear it thundering several miles away.

Symonds Yat is where the River Wye collides with two limestone cliffs forming a gorge. The river narrows, because of the cliffs, and subsequently gathers speed, crashing against the cliff sides and making an echoing noise like a huge waterfall.

As we were getting very close to SY, I signalled to the lads that I needed to empty my canoe again. Unusually, this time they all came to the bank, to make a toilet break!!!

Then, we all got back into our canoes and paddled in single file round the corner to tackle our demon. We left good gaps between each kayak and this time I went first. Not because I was the best canoeist or the bravest, but if any kayak was going to disintegrate in these rapids, it was likely to mine.

So, with mouth dry, and heart pounding I set out into the middle of the river, gulped, and then paddled forcefully around the corner. The booming crescendo of water noise was deafening. The river was crashing against the limestone walls and then rebounding back and over the heads of any canoeist stupid enough to tackle it.

I just paddled hard and fixed my stare down the centre tunnel created by the rebounding waves. About twenty or so strokes and I was hurled out the other side, safe and unharmed. I swung my canoe around to watch the escapades of the rest of the group. As each one came through unscathed, a sheer look of terror quickly evaporated into a huge smile of enormous relief. To a man, every one punched the air as their fears disappeared. Symonds Yat conquered; but to be fair it was not as demanding and dangerous as most of the rapids that we had already tackled, because there were no rocks at all down the centre channel – it just looked and sounded horrendous.

After Symonds the river widened and became slow again. The paddling was now hard, we were all tired, so we were very pleased that our next campsite was only a short distance away. Suddenly, I yelled to Benoit, "Look at that," and there lying in the shallows, sunning itself, was that night's meal. I had been a coarse fisherman for years; often using spinners to trap my prey. I had caught plenty of Perch, but the big fish that I was after never appeared. Now, suddenly, I see my first live Pike just inches away in the slow water of the Wye. I cracked it over the head with my paddle as I passed and shouted to the next boat behind me. "Pull that out of the water, Sheds. It's tonight's dinner"

Sheds paddled to the side, and after a bit of a struggle managed to pull the dead fish up and across the bows of his canoe. It was a hefty beast, I would estimate just over two feet long, and, bulky enough to feed all of us.

Sheds paddled across to me to let me see our catch, when, suddenly it tremored, flicked its tail, and in a flash was back in the water, stunned but still able to rapidly swim away.

Egg and beans for dinner, again!!!

The River, now, was very brackish, slow and tidal. So paddling was tedious. We were all really pleased when we made our last night's camp at Monmouth.

After pitching our tents and eating, we fell in with tradition and went into town for a drink. The first pub we went into was a very traditional, spit & sawdust sort of place. It would do for the first pint – especially as we were all gagging after working hard on the River.

We split into two rounds of four, and I was first up for my group.

"Four pints of your best bitter please, barman."

No reaction from the man behind the bar. He continued to talk in Welsh to other customers at the far end of the bar,

So I raised my voice so that he could definitely hear.

"Excuse me! Four pints of your best bitter please, barman."

He still ignored me, so I walked part way down the bar and said. "I know you understand, because I heard you all speaking English when we walked in. Your posters are all in English, too!!!"

Reluctantly, he turned towards me, with a scowl on his face, which illustrated that we were not welcome. He poured the four pints without saying a word, and took my money. I deliberately counted my change in front of him, before I moved away with the drinks. We also stayed there, again deliberately, for the night. We didn't have any problem getting served again. The locals were still unfriendly, but I guess they didn't want to stir it up with us – they had probably heard on the grapevine that we were all SAS!!!

Next morning we were all up bright and early, and excited. Even though this trip had been epic, we were all looking forward to getting back to College and sleeping in our own beds. So, although it was hard work paddling, we really put some muscle into it and caught up with the tailenders of the main group. We dragged the canoes up the bank at Tintern Abbey, but this time unloaded them of tents, sleeping bags, etc, and put them straight onto the trailers. This was all supervised by Charlie, our PE technician, while our PE lecturers were acting as chefs and waiters at the barbecue that they had waiting for us.

Brilliant!

*   *   *

Most of us slept the four hours it took to drive slowly back to College.

When we got there, Benoit had a surprise waiting for him. We all rushed off to see the girlfriends that we hadn't seen for seven days, but Benny had a note pinned to his door from his.

"That b*****d, while we've been away, Dave Bloody Dingle has been having it away with my girl. I'm gonna kill him!!!"

He turned to go looking for Dingle.

"Hey, steady on Benny," I warned him; *being unusually cautious for me!* "If you do anything stupid, you'll get kicked out of College. End of teaching career."

"Bugger the teaching career. He's asked for this."

I grabbed his arm to restrain him, and said, "There are other ways. We won't let him off the hook, but there are other ways to go about it without ditching your career.

"Like what?"

"Dunno yet, but I'll think of something."

David Dingle was the most disliked member of the first year PE students. He was a tennis player, who was alright at that, but he didn't like getting his hands dirty. So, consequently, when it came to rock climbing, canoeing, rugby, etc., out came the crepe bandage and the predictable sprained wrist stopped him taking part in these sessions.

His theory marks were high, so he was going to pass most courses on the strength of that, without taking part in much of the practical side. He was going to become a 'paper' PE teacher, who would no doubt, in future, admonish pupils who came to him with a note to excuse them from his lessons. – The worst kind of hypocrite. But worse than that – Benoit's girlfriend had now left him after being wooed by this scumbag while we were all away completing *our* practical course!

Benny had some harsh words with his ex-girlfriend and told her to tell Dingle that he'd better stay well clear of him, but that was as far as it went.

Meanwhile, we let the dust settle for a few weeks before we put into action the plan that we had hatched.

Bulmershe was a fairly progressive College, but still had a rule that students had to return to their own rooms in the Halls of Residence by midnight. Tony Milburn, one of our PE lecturers and the warden of Dave Dingle's hostel, was a stickler for the rules.

We also knew that Dingle, like most students, ignored this rule, and his new girlfriend often stayed all night with him. If caught he would be up on a 'disciplinary' and could get kicked out of College (dependant on his record).

So, 3 weeks after our Wye trip return, Benny and myself put the plan into action. We left it until three in the morning, so that everybody was snoozing away, before setting out on phase one of our plan.

Benny borrowed a set of ladders from the caretakers usual storage point, while I went upstairs to the first floor of the hostel and in the darkness, silently removed the outside door handle from Dingles room by torchlight.

Meanwhile Benny had arrived back with the ladders and, again silently, placed them below Dingles open quarterlight window while I ran the fire hose out to him. Benoit then climbed the ladder, fastened the hose to the window-stay with the wire coat hanger that he'd brought with him, and turned on. Just before we sprinted back to our own rooms, I hit the fire alarm.

All Hell was breaking loose across the way at the other hostel while we were just re-entering ours, locking our doors and frantically getting into bed. After about twenty minutes the anticipated banging sounded on our doors.

"What the Hell is going on?" I yelled as I went to open the door.

There stood a purple faced Tony Milburn, foaming at the mouth *(I don't blame him)* screaming, "What do you know about this, Masters?"

"Hang on a minute," I said VERY irately, "First of all, I don't know what you are talking about, and secondly, it is nearly four o'clock in the morning. Whatever it is that I don't know about *should* have waited until tomorrow. I have lectures to attend, and I need my sleep!"

"If there's nothing else, Mr. Milburn, I'll try and rescue what is left of my night!"

I turned to shut the door, but Mr. Milburn jammed his foot in the door and yelled, "I know you're behind this Masters, and when I prove it you'll be kicked out of this College."

I felt like saying 'prove it' but merely settled for "Goodnight Mr. Milburn. I'll see you in the morning!"

Over his shoulder I could see Pedro, Squalor, Honey, Rico and Brum all giggling away. I knew Benoit hadn't said anything to them as we had both sworn a vow of silence, even to our mates, over this incident.

In the College Refectory, the following morning at breakfast the lads were buzzing with questions. Benny and myself, just fended them off saying that after the bar we'd decided to have a game of cards and then an early night. So I could vouch for him, and he for me.

Pedro then said, "I know you're lying, Jimbo, 'cos when Milburn knocked on your door, you came out wearing pyjamas. -

You never wear pyjamas. You were expecting him!"

"It was a cold night" I retorted, "I only sleep in the buff when it's warm."

Pedro looked at me quizzically, and smirked, he knew, they all knew, but they also knew that they were going to get nothing out of me and Benny.

Shortly after that the summer term ended and I went off to my holiday job with British Steel (more about that in chapter nine).

When we returned as second year students this incident was forgotten – but not by Benny. Unfortunately, Dingle's girlfriend had also decided to take an early night that night, so wasn't in his room. Although he had been admonished for being at the root of this problem, he was still in College, and Benoit felt that justice still hadn't been done.

Dingle, hard faced it in every PE practical after that, but he knew we hadn't finished with him.

Chapter 7

Life Off Campus

The first obstacle to overcome in my second year at Bulmershe was living off campus. There was only enough accommodation in 'Halls' for first and final year students, so I ended up living in Twyford, four miles from College as the crow flies, but six miles by road.

Twyford was a sleepy little village, just off the M4 in Berkshire, hardly any cars went through there, except for the time we had a female flasher.

A young(ish) lady was seen quite regularly walking through the Village, wearing a fur coat and stillettos. Every time a car passed she would open the coat to reveal that she was wearing nothing else apart for these two items.

Suddenly, our sleepy little village was experiencing traffic jams for the first time ever, as traffic was diverting from the M4 to pass through.

How on earth did they all know about it, it wasn't on the news, and it was before home computers, facebook & twitter!

Extra police were drafted in to cope with the traffic.

I lived in Twyford for a year and never saw her once, but all of the other ladies of the village stopped wearing their fur coats, during that period, just in case they were suspected!!!

I liked the accommodation that I shared with Rico, Brian and Brum, which was a granny flat built onto the side of a fake Tudor four bedroomed house, but I didn't stay there very often, as it interfered with my social life at College too much.

The last 'College' bus to Twyford went at 8 pm from the campus, otherwise I could walk two miles to the A4 and catch a later 'corporation' bus at 10pm. The College bar closed at 11pm.

On a couple of occasions, I left early to get the bus, but leaving at 9.15 pm, to walk two miles to catch it hardly seemed worth the effort.

Another couple of times I waited until the bar chucked out and walked the six miles home – but that was also a lot of effort.

So, eventually, I did what all of the other fine upstanding second year students did, and found myself a first year girlfriend that had a room.

Alan, our Second Team hooker, told me about a particular girl that he fancied, but was having difficulties with. Everytime he wanted to take her out somewhere, her mate had to tag along – would I help him out and make a foursome?

I asked him what she was like, and when he only said 'alright', I feared the worst. So, he suggested we invite ourselves for a coffee, and I could judge for myself.

We called at their hostel, and sure enough, Alan's prospective date was there with Annie, I looked at the two of them, both decent lookers, but I thought that I was getting the better of the two.

We arranged to go out for a drink in a foursome two days later, and after that Annie and myself starting seeing each other on a regular basis.

Poor Alan, managed to find me a girlfriend, but still didn't manage to get fixed up himself. Once Annie and I were an item, Alan's date went to the next College disco, and left that night with a young rocker from Reading.

My relationship with Annie was one of the most fiery that I've ever had. We were always arguing, and as a result I regularly found my bags put outside her door, or my books & notes floating down from her third floor window.

On these occasions, I slept on the floor of whoever from the Rugby team had space available, but sometimes if our disagreements began after everyone else had gone to sleep, I had nowhere to go. So, I either walked, or found somewhere else to sleep. Then I hit on a plan!

The Hostel Wardens always checked the common rooms & corridors for 'illegal' occupants, but I don't think they checked the bathrooms. So one night I tested it out. I took half a dozen seat cushions from the Common Room, used them to pad out the bottom of a bath, and spent a fairly comfortable, trouble free night's sleep.

This worked fine, when I had nowhere to sleep, for a couple of months, but then, one night, I was sleeping restlessly, turning over regularly. Accidentally, and unknowingly, I knocked open the cold tap with one of my feet. The bath started to fill up. The foam seat cushions acted like a sponge, and in a very short time my dreams turned into a nightmare in which I was drowning. It was a cold night, middle of winter, and I was soaking wet and freezing. Fortunately, I had a my PE holdall with me, so dried on my towel, and changed into my tracksuit, etc. It was four o'clock in the morning, so now the dilemma was – do I try to get back to sleep somewhere else, or walk back to Twyford, just in time for breakfast, and to catch the College bus back to where I had just come from. I decided on the latter.

At breakfast I chatted with my other 'flat-mates', who were all very surprised to see me. Brian, who was the only one with a car, offered me a lift in future, but he always left College between 7.and 8 pm, so that he could write up his coursework. I thanked him, but preferred to do (or often, not do) my essays in the College Library, and then hit the bar at 8. Brum, likewise, could give me a lift, he had a Vespa scooter, but I would have to leave early AND buy a crash helmet. I told them that in future I would walk, as I did that night.

Brum then said, "Well, I think you're stupid, walking six miles down the roads. It is much quicker to come through the woods, it cuts two miles off the journey. There's a road that cuts right through the middle, and leads almost to the back gate of this house."

"Mind you, I drove home last Wednesday, and nearly fell off my bike. I saw the biggest rat I've ever seen in my life, under the railway bridge. Fortunately as I got closer my headlights and engine noise scared him off."

"Well that doesn't bother me," I replied full of bravado, "The woods will be full of rats, but they're more scared of us than we are of them. I'll just make plenty of noise as I approach the bridge."

It was only a week later, that I had the opportunity to test out this theory. It was just before midnight when I left the Students Union Bar. Even though it was cold, I walked at a good pace and covered the two miles to the wood in no time at all, and in a bit of a sweat due to my speed. The wood was about a mile wide, and although there was a good single track tarmac road going through it, there was no lighting. My eyes quickly adjusted to the darkness, and although I could neither see or hear any of the wood's residents, I whistled loudly just in case they saw me. I was almost completely through the wood when I saw the outline of the railway bridge come into view. I started to whistle louder, my eyes were like saucers, as I got nearer and nearer the monster rat's hangout.

SUDDENLY, a train came rattling loudly across the track overhead!!!

That was it!!! Bravado dissolved - my knees came up to my chin, my arms pumped like pistons as I sprinted the last mile for home. Sebastian Coe and Steve Ovett definitely wouldn't have kept up with me, *and I was carrying a holdall full of PE kit*!!!

*   *   *

Needless to say, I didn't walk back to lodgings through the wood again.

So, next time it was back to the corporation bus or a hard floor again.

On several occasions, I left the bar too late and missed the last bus so had a further 4 miles to walk. Then, as regular as clockwork, as I was walking along, minding my own business, with my holdall slung over my shoulder, a police car would pull up.

"Where are you going at this time of night?"

"Twyford. Missed the last bus."

"What's in your bag?"

"PE kit and books – I'm a student at Bulmershe."

"Would you mind emptying everything out onto the pavement?"

I gave a huge sigh, and looked at him as if to say *you must be joking*.

He glared back at me to suggest that he wasn't.

"OK – tracksuit, trainers, socks, sociology book, psychology book . . ."

When it was all on the flags, I said, "That's it."

He then took the holdall from me and searched inside to make sure nothing else was concealed, and then said, "OK, sorry about that, son, but this is a high burglary area, and you are dressed all in black carrying a big bag . . ."

He didn't need to say any more, "It's OK, you're only doing your job," I said, honestly. I seriously wasn't bothered, he *was* only doing his job. Besides it broke up an otherwise very boring walk home.

It was when the same thing happened to me three times that month that I WAS bothered. . .

". . . What's in your bag?"

"Same as last time – you only stopped me three weeks ago."

"And what would that be?"

"Surely you remember, it was only three weeks ago. I'm a student at Bulmershe College."

"So, what would a student from Bulmershe College be carrying in his bag?"

"Same as last time – surely you remember!"

"I've got a short memory"

"Bloody well must have!"

"Do I have to arrest you and take you down the nick to see what's inside your bag?"

"Is your nick towards Twyford or that way?"

"No, son, it's that way another four miles into Reading."

"And if you take me into Reading and then find you've arrested an innocent man, are you going to give me a lift back to Twyford?"

"No, son, I AM NOT!"

"OK - tracksuit, trainers, socks, sociology book, psychology book . . ."

I was pissed off this time.

I didn't walk back to lodgings again.

However, *(always thinking)*, I did hatch another plan.

I couldn't afford a car like Brian's, but what about a scooter, *again*, like Brum's?

There was a 'Bike' Shop in Wokingham, so on the next occasion that I was there, I checked it out. They didn't sell scooters but I did buy myself a nice 100cc Yamaha, on HP, from them.

Now, if I had no early morning lectures, I could have a lie in rather than catch the early morning 'College' bus or alternatively I could leave at the same time for early lectures but return home when I wanted.

That was in theory, because I soon became the laughing stock of the rest of my flatmates as I pushed the Yamaha up and down our snow clad road while they were all warm inside their little bus.

Of course, I took the bike back to the shop to complain, and they pointed out that I had been flooding the engine. - Some 'wally' of a previous owner had put the petrol switch on back to front when he had repaired it! So when I was turning the fuel off each night . . . !

The next problem I encountered with this – cursed – motorbike was when one day, I had gone to College and (honestly this time) told one of my lecturers that I had completed the assignment, but that I had left it at my lodgings six miles away. I'd already had a two week extension on producing this essay, so he warned me that I only had until 4.30 pm, when he was going home, to get it to him! It was already 12.30 and I had lectures all afternoon.

So, undeterred, I jumped on my motorbike and throttled it the six miles to Twyford.

I saw the speed cop approaching, before he clocked me. I slowed down to 35 mph and looked through my wing mirrors to witness him doing a U turn behind me. His big Honda caught me up in no time.

"Going a bit fast there weren't you, son?"

"It's a 40 limit on this road, isn't it?" I replied with as much innocence in my voice as I could muster.

"Both you and I know that you were doing well over 40."

Well, I knew it was one thing him thinking that, but proving it was a different matter, so I said innocently again, "Well, I wasn't watching the speedo, officer, I suppose I might have touched 39 at some stage."

He raised his eyebrows and smirked. "With an accent like that you're not from round here, are you? What are you doing in Reading?"

"No, I'm from Middlesbrough, but I'm studying at Bulmershe to be a teacher. I have to get this essay back there in the next half hour"

"D'you know, I haven't been to Middlesbrough for about thirty years now. In fact I haven't been back home to Newcastle for ten."

"Oh, you're a Geordie, then" I replied, glad to have got the subject away from my speeding, but desperately keen to get back to College. "You wouldn't recognise the Boro now. Everytime I go home they've built something new or changed streets into one way. I don't know where I am."

"I know it's the same with me, young fella. Anyway I could reminisce all day, but have to get on. Keep your speed down. It's better to arrive safely than not at all."

"Cheers, mate, I will," I said, tongue in cheek, and then set off, slowly.

I managed to make afternoon lectures, AND get the assignment in on time. But after all that I still only got a D+ for the essay. My tutor said that it was downgraded for being late *and for being copied from another student*!

Cheek!!!

*   *   *

There were a couple more mishaps that occurred with the motorbike later in the year, but before I got to them, my College year had started pretty well and my rugby with Reading looked set for another memorable Season.

Pre-season I was selected to play in a commemorative match for The Rest of Berkshire against Newbury. I think the selectors looked on this as an opportunity to test me out against some stiff opposition as up to now, with Reading, I'd had things pretty easy.

Nobody told me that the Newbury captain, and open side flanker who was marking me, David Anderson, had only the previous season, played an outstanding game against the New Zealand All Blacks for the Southern Counties.

Just as well I suppose, because if that wasn't bad enough, when I arrived at the ground, I discovered that our captain and my scrum half, Dave Spofforth, had pulled out injured at the last moment, and as they didn't have a replacement scrum half they drafted in a flanker as a stop gap. This stop gap almost had me killed, as right from his first pass, which came to me lobbed and slow, I was flattened by Anderson. At the next scrum I moved a bit closer to my half back colleague so that he could get the ball to me more easily – unfortunately it also meant I was closer to Anderson. I got the ball away to our centre – but it didn't matter – as a good two seconds later, the man flattened me again in a late tackle – *but no whistle from the ref.* The man was a maniac, and he looked like one. His blonde comb-over hairstyle had now come forward all over his face, his front teeth were missing, and there was fire in his eyes. The referee wasn't helping and for the first time ever in a rugby match I was scared. Anderson continued to hit me in late tackles, tackles off the ball, elbows to my face, etc. I had no alternative.

At the next scrum I deliberately stood in even closer so that I could get the ball away quickly, and when the inevitable late tackle came in I was ready. I pulled my best haymaker punch from somewhere near my knees and caught the flanker full in the face. I knew that he would probably half kill me in the resultant fight – but at least the referee would now have to warn us both - and keep an eye on us for future bad conduct!

The plan didn't work! Anderson merely rolled over on top of me, after my best punch had decked him. Then, unnervingly he simply smiled at me, tussled my hair, and said, "I wondered when you'd try that lad."

As he ran away laughing, I just sank to my knees and thought *"That's it, I'm dead,- I'm dead!"*

Fortunately, at the very next scrum our stop gap half back injured himself, and our captain asked if there was anybody in the team who could play scrum half. My hand went up like a shot – it wasn't my favourite position, but at least now I'd have someone else thumping me instead of David Anderson.

The rest of the match, thank God, was uneventful. I was happy to trot off the field rather than be carried on a stretcher, to have a beautifully relaxing hot bath, and then enter the bar for the after match drinks.

In there, I chatted with Spofforth, another Northerner, who I knew from playing against him for College. We laughed and joked about all sorts – not least the pummelling I'd received out on the pitch. "Then he said, "Let's eat," and we went into a room next door where a glorious buffet was spread out on what was obviously a covered over snooker table. I was just munching on my second chicken leg, when a door at the end creaked open, and the

Selection Committee members entered the room.

"What are you doing eating the Committee's buffet?" the leading old fart asked.

"Well, I was just . . . I was told . . ." I stuttered and looked around for Spoff, but the crafty Tyke had set me up, and disappeared.

I dragged my tail back into the bar to be confronted by a smiling Dave Spofforth and his very smart well dressed gentleman friend.

I snapped at the former, "Next time I play against you , Spoff, I'm gonna knock your f*****g teeth out !"

He just laughed and replied, "Never mind that, this gentleman wants to buy you a drink."

I felt a bit better knowing that, so turned to look at the generous stranger.

He was dressed in a well tailored, expensive looking light grey suit, with a pink shirt and maroon tie. His hair was neatly combed across from left to right with a tiny quiff, and he had a gleaming smile.

"What would you like?" he asked as he gestured to the barman. "I think I owe you one after the hard time I gave you in the game."

Bloody Hell!!! It was David Anderson with his hair combed and his teeth in, he looked human!

Who was it that said "Rugby was a hooligan's game played by gentlemen?"

Whoever it was I think he was right.

Needless to say, I DIDN'T get selected for the County again.

Especially, after the next bombshell had hit me. One of our College lecturers, who also coached the Rugby Team, came to see me at the end of a basketball session in the sportshall, and asked me, "Who are you playing for this season, Jimbo?"

"Reading, the same as last," was my reply.

"Well that might be a bad move, 'cos your grades, and attendance and discipline aren't up to scratch. And there are some lecturers that want you out."

(I knew he meant Tony Milburn)

"I'm fighting hard to keep you in, but the only thing going for you is your rugby. If you come back and play for College, that might just swing it, because when the third years go out on teaching practice, they want you to take over the captaincy.

That will definitely look good on your record."

I didn't know if Bob Richards was bulling me, but could I take the risk? I desperately wanted to play for Reading again that season, but could I risk letting my Mum down by being kicked out of College. Two other PE students had been given the boot at the end of the first year, perhaps it was my turn.

Realistically, I had no alternative. I played my rugby that year for College.

My captaincy of the team went down on my record, but didn't last long. In my third match as leader, we played RAF Brize Norton in a hastily arranged match when both teams had a blank weekend.

We were met on arrival by their Commanding Officer, who said in a very plumy, typically RAF voice, "I'd like to thank you chaps for coming," as he shook my hand. We're in the RAF Cup Final next week, and we desperately needed a work out before that game."

"Well, I hope we can give you a good game," I replied as I shook his hand back, and entered the changing rooms.

When we went 15 – 0 up after just ten minutes, the C.O. was livid, yelling and cursing, and purple in the face. At half time, when we were leading by 36 points he was nowhere to be seen.

"Right Lads," I said in the half time huddle. "This lot aren't up to much. We might as well get a decent work out for ourselves, and work on some of our set moves that we've practiced. At least they'll be a bit more than passive opposition. We'll run the ball, as normal, in loose play, but from scrums and lineouts we'll call a move." Everybody nodded, but our outside centre had different ideas. He was our top scorer, and was big headed enough to think that because of that *he* should have been made Captain.

I was big headed enough to know that he was only top scorer because I kept setting him up so well!

At the very first scrum of the second half, I called for a 'scissors'. Tommy had to run across his winger and give him the ball running in the other direction. Easy enough but effective. However, when the ball got to Tommy he simply side stepped his opponent, and ran in a try from 40 metres.

I was livid.

When he came back to the halfway line with his beaming smile, I tersely snapped at him, "I called a scissors on that ball. **Do it** next time."

"We didn't need it"

"I don't care if we needed it or not. It was called so we can get something useful out of this game."

"What's the point?"

That was it. I'd snapped. I was purple in the face when I yelled, "What's the point? What's the point? - Listen, big head, we can all run in tries all day against this lot. They're too easy. We've won the game. Now let's get something useful out of it!"

"But . . ."

Now we were nose to nose, "No but's, I'm captain of this team, now just do it, if you want to play for us again."

"You can't . . . "

It was at this point that the referee, realising that a fight was about to break out, stepped in.

"Hey, lads, everybody's waiting to restart the game."

I spun on the ref, still livid, and said, "I want him sent off."

The ref, bewildered (never having had a situation like this before), squeakily retorted, "I can't do that! He's on your team."

"What if I punch his teeth down his throat then?"

"Then you'll get sent off for fighting."

Tommy smirked.

I grabbed him by the collar, and said, "We'll settle this back at College."

By the time we arrived back at College, I'd had a shower and a couple of pints, and time to think. The lads had, individually, spoken to me. One at a time, they pledged their support, but also told me to not do anything silly, as it wasn't worth losing my career over this egotistical b*****d.

So, I sat, at the back of the coach home, and Tommy sat at the front. We only spoke once, on the way off the bus I told him, "There will be a Disciplinary Committee called over this matter."

"Fine," was all he replied.

The Disciplinary Committee meeting was held and both sides of the disagreement were aired. They went into a huddle and decided that they didn't want to lose their top scorer – nor did they want to lose their Captain, so we should sort out our differences and play together as team-mates.

Again livid, I said. "So he gets no punishment at all for disobeying and starting an argument with the Team Captain?"

The Chairman simply raised his eyebrows and looked at the ceiling.

"Well, thanks for your support fellas. You'd better look for another Captain. I am not willing to do the job with one hand tied behind my back, especially with a prat like Herrington in the team."

Nobody gave a reply, they all silently nodded.

"And, one last thing:- if the next captain you appoint IS Herrington, then I will definitely be playing for Reading for the rest of this season!"

So, my College captaincy had lasted 3 games. The next captain they appointed was Keith, a quiet lad, well respected, and placid. No likely flare ups there then!!!

I suppose the main highlight of the season after that was that I was invited to attend a young England Development Camp under Don Rutherford at Bisham Abbey.

* * *

As you would probably expect by now, things at College didn't go down without their little hiccups either. In a previous chapter, I explained how the County Council, in their wisdom had amalgamated our College with Easthampsted Girls College and, how we fellas didn't mind having the extra female influx. We'll that also came with its drawbacks, because as well as this intake of students, we were also obliged to find jobs for their staff.

I was horrified when I found out that my timetable for my second term included one hour of National Dance per week.

Now, this is OK for the students, male or female, that would probably teach this subject to their pupils at their future schools, but in my case it was never going to happen. Normally, topics like these would be made optional, counterbalanced against something like weight training or circuit training or distance running, but this subject was compulsory. There could only be one possible explanation for this; one of the Easthampstead Park lecturers had to be found a job, and she could only teach National Dance.

I wasn't happy, it was my education that was being compromised here.

So, to be fair to this lady, I didn't give her a chance. I attended my first seminar with an attitude.

She greeted us, explained that we were going to learn the national dance of a different country each week, and that we should come appropriately attired for that week.

I asked her what she meant.

"At the end of each session, I will tell you which country's dance we are covering in the following session, so that you can come in that country's national costume, or else wear whatever you would normally dance in."

That was the green light for me.

The following week was the Tarantella, the national dance of Italy. I came dressed in a blue & white checked Ben Sherman shirt and short jeans held up over my black bovver boots with a pair of broad red braces.

Mrs. Baxter, our lecturer almost fainted. "What do you think you are doing coming into this session dressed like that?"

"Last week. I specifically asked you what we should dress in for this session, you said either the national costume of Italy, or whatever you would normally dance in. This is what I would normally dance in."

The rest of the students fell about laughing. Mrs Baxter merely said, "Young man, I think you have deliberately misinterpreted what I said. Next time you turn up inappropriately attired, you will be sent out to change."

I replied, "Whatever . . ." and turned to my laughing colleagues to get on with my stamping out of the Tarantella.

At the end of the session we were told to come appropriately attired, (*she eyeballed me*), for the National Dance of Scotland.

The following week, everybody came appropriately dressed. I didn't this time overstep the boundaries, I dressed in a black vest and black gymnastics trousers, tastefully tucked in, I thought, to a pair of tartan, Bay City Rollers socks.

As the session commenced, and we were being taught the Highland Fling, we accompanied it by voluminous whoops and yells (as the Scots do), only to be told after a while to tone it down, as we were going too far. So we obliged, we changed to calling each other 'Mac' at every opportunity, in broad Scottish accents.

"Could I have the next dance, MacSqualor?" asked MacRico

"You're looking mighty fine today, MacPedro", complimented McHoney.

As we were talking, the President of the Student's Union, Haroon Khan, walked past the window. "Oh look," MacBenoit pointed out, "there's MacHaroon!"

Everybody fell about laughing.

But, it was **me** that was kicked out of the class for disrupting the session.

I had to report to the Head of PE, affectionately known as Big Bill as he was only about 4 foot eleven tall. I told him my grievances, in particular that I objected to having my time and education wasted by having to take part in a pastime that I had no intention of teaching, purely to find employment for a lady who should simply have been given early retirement. Big Bill, didn't say anything about that (but didn't disagree either – which spoke volumes) he merely told me that if I wanted to pass the course, I would need to attend future sessions, and that to do so I needed to write a formal apology to the Dance Lecturer, promising that there would not be a repeat of this kind of behaviour. I guessed, from the twinkle in Bill's eyes, that he was secretly on my side in this matter, but that he, too, had his hands tied.

So, I wrote out an apology and duplicated it twice. One copy had to go to Mrs. Baxter, one to Big Bill, and one had to be pinned, for public display, on the PE noticeboard. I complied with these stipulations, but not before I had gone around every member of the second year PE students, showing them the letter but pointing out that I didn't mean a word.

*   *   *

The very last act of my second year at Bulmershe resulted in disaster too.

I had decided that, even though my motorbike was very small and liable to overheat, it would be more useful to me in Middlesbrough for the eight weeks summer holiday, than it would being put into storage in Reading. Also, if I hitch-hiked home (or went by public transport) I could only take one bag. This way I could save money, and take all my washing home for Mum to do!

So, on the fateful morning of my departure, I loaded up the bike with three hefty bags and stuffed a map inside my windcheater. The holdall that I used as my main college bag was far too long to fit on the small luggage rack, so I used my elastic bungee ties to strap it to the pillion passenger seat as well. On top of that went two smaller bags (but not much smaller) as well. The bonus was, that these bags provided quite a comfortable back rest for me, too.

From behind you could just about see my crash helmet peeping over the top.

I set out for Oxford at about 10 am, I had decided to go the more direct route, up the middle of the Country, on A roads because not only was it shorter, but as a learner driver, I was barred from using motorways. I estimated that by this route and the slower pace of my bike, that the 260 mile journey would take about eight hours. How wrong I was!!!

I arrived in Middlesbrough thirteen hours later, due to a couple of mishaps.

Firstly, when I approached any junction that lead onto a motorway, I looked for the signs that indicated the diversion for vehicles that were banned from the motorway. This worked fine until I got to Leicester. The signs led me away from the motorway towards the town centre and then stopped. I spent more than an hour trying to extricate myself from that town, and after a frustrating and fuel sapping two hours, eventually found my way to the A1 via the A46 dual carriageway.

I definitely nominate Leicester as being the worst signposted town in Britain!

I hadn't travelled much further north, when I discovered the need for a toilet stop and a cup of coffee. Darkness had fallen, and even though it had been a bright and sunny July day, the evening temperature was becoming quite cold.

After another mile, or two, I spotted my refuge. In a layby at the side of the road was a truckers' stop – with toilets! I had expected to have to dive behind a hedge!

So, I pulled in. Went to the grotty toilet and washed my face and hands with lovely warm water, to wake and warm myself up. Then at the counter I asked 'mine host' for a bacon buttie and a large mug of coffee.

We chatted, and I told him of my ordeal, and how freezing cold I was becoming. He told me of an old trick he used to use when he was a biker. He gave me an old newspaper that he had behind the counter, and I returned to the toilets to insulate the front of my body with lashings of The Daily Mirror.

I walked back to the counter like a robot, but I was warm! I picked up my helmet, thanked him and returned to my bike in the lay-by.

Once I'd started the bike, shuffled around a bit to get all of the headlines in the right place, I glanced in my wing mirror and over my shoulder, saw the gap in the traffic, leaned my bike over, and was off!

Or not off, as the case may be!!!

As I leaned over, all the bags slipped. The bike (and me) were dragged to the ground. The bags jammed under the Yamaha and it was left on its side, propped up in the air, with its back wheel spinning. I was laid out, sideways, still in the driving position.

The truckers' peed themselves laughing. I didn't look at them, but could hear their taunts, as I repositioned the bags on my luggage rack, before setting off again.

I arrived home, as already mentioned, thirteen hours later, at 11 pm.
My mother was beside herself with worry, as she had expected me hours earlier. In those days before mobile phones, I had no way of letting her know I would be late.

I crawled the bike into Laycock Street, worried that to add to my problems I was going to run out of petrol, and stopped outside of our front door. I dismounted the Yamaha with great difficulty and walked towards the door like a hunchback. All of my muscles had frozen and cramped, and after thirteen hours, I couldn't straighten up.
I scrambled to get out my key, and place it into the lock. My Mum heard the commotion, and came to let me in.

After the inevitable inquest, and a hot meal, I got into my own, extremely comfortable bed, and slept for twelve hours!

Next day, after breakfast, I remembered that I needed fuel, and rode my bike towards the nearest petrol station that was only 600 metres away.

Then, after over 300 miles of *almost* trouble free riding, I crashed into a car, at the top of Laycock Street!!! As a dopey old man in a beat up Jaguar drove around the corner, on my side of the road, I slammed into it, and wrecked my bike!

I was lucky, though, not to injure myself, as I was bending around the corner, I saw him at the last moment and realised that at that angle I was going to go under the car's front, so I straightened up. The Yammie slammed into his bumper and ejected me over the roof of the Jag.

Now I don't know if it was my PE training or what, but I instinctively tucked into a ball as I cleared the car, and after a double somersault went bouncing down the road, shaken but hardly marked. I was so badly shaken by the events, though, that my hands were trembling to such an extent that I couldn't get my helmet off.

An old lady came forward to help. "Here you are, son, let me do it for you."

In a couple of seconds she had released the clip and as she removed the helmet squealed, "Oh my God, it our Jim!!!"

The old lady was me Mam.

I never did ride that bike again, I repaired it and sold it.

Chapter 8

My Final Year

Fortunately, I didn't need my motorbike in my third year at Bulmershe because I was once again living in 'Halls' on campus. Besides it was easier, quicker and much cheaper to hitch-hike home at term's end.

My social life once again became very hectic, but also, as this was my final year, so did my academic life. I was having to work harder on assignments, theses and seminars, but the first obstacle to overcome was my final Teaching Practice. Not that this worried me too greatly, I've always been a confident teacher that got on well with the kids, but on this occasion I was allocated a school in Slough that they hadn't used for four years because it was so rough. Additionally, just to make a real test of it, my supervising tutor was Mrs.Baxter !!!

A bit naughty of them, but I can understand the logic behind it. Blandford Secondary was going to make or break one of us. If I could cope with teaching at this school with this tutor, I would be able to cope anywhere. If Mrs Baxter could cope with me . . . well she deserved a medal – she would have certainly have proved her worth, and if she couldn't cope with me, then they might have forced her resignation. Either way it was a win – win situation for College.

Of course, I wasn't informed beforehand by the College that this was the roughest school on their books, it was just hearsay by the older students. So, I thought they were just trying to wind me up. It didn't take long for me to find out they weren't!

On only my second day in the school, I was timetabled for a basketball lesson with 4C.

"OK lads," I shouted at them whilst standing on one of the benches in the changing rooms, "I'm Mr. Masters, and I'm going to be taking you for basketball for the next eight weeks. As soon as you've changed come to the staff changingroom for a ball. Take it into the Sportshall and practice shooting at one of the side baskets."

Of course, the keen lads changed quickly and did as I asked, allowing me more time to cajole the slow coaches into moving faster.

"Come on fellas, it'll be dinnertime before you're ready at this rate. I don't want to *have to* give up my dinnertime keeping you in a detention to teach you how to change more quickly!"

That worked. Suddenly these unkeen slowcoaches moved up a couple of gears and were soon jogging into the basketball arena.

As soon as I walked into the sportshall, I blew my whistle. "Right lads, that'll do. Sit on the benches and we'll sort out what we're doing this lesson."

Twenty nine pupils responded to the command, but one boy kept shooting at a side basket.

"Hey, son, we're ready to start the lesson," I shouted much louder.

No response, he just kept shooting.

So I turned to the class and asked "Has he a problem with his hearing?"

Almost as a unit, they replied, "It's Billy Mackay, Sir"

"I don't care who it is." I spun on my heels and yelled, "Oi, Mackay, we are ready to start, come and sit on this bench."

This time I got a response. He turned to look at me and with a snarl said, "I don't need to take any notice of you, you're not even a real teacher."

Bad move. He'd got me riled.

Fortunately, I was 15 metres away, and by the time I strode forcefully towards him, I'd had time to think. "Oh, because I'm a student, you think I can't teach you anything?"

"Probably not, none of the others ever have!"

"So that must mean, you think you know more than me! You must be a better sportsman than me."

"Probably."

"OK," I retorted, "Name any sport that you think you're better at than me, and I'll take you on at it. - If you beat me, you take the lesson and do anything you want."

"You don't mean it."

"There are twenty nine witnesses sitting on that bench." I turned once again to face the rest of the class. "Did you lad's all hear that? I promise that if Billy Mackay can beat me at any sport, he can choose what we do in this lesson."

Then I looked back at the disruptive pupil, and said, "Come on then, Mackay, what's your best sport?"

I was hoping he wasn't going to say Judo, or Table Tennis, but he obliged me with, "Football, innit.," as he smiled broadly at the rest of the class and shrugged his shoulders, in a clever cock fashion.

"OK, Mackay, football it is then.

Put your basketball over there with the rest, while I go and get a football."

I jogged towards the PE staffroom, and as I entered the Head of PE, a stocky Welshman called Dewi Thomas, hardly looked up from the reports he was writing.

"Just want a football," I said. "Change of plan."

"OK," he said and got back to writing.

I took the ball and jogged back to the class, thinking *'this is my first lesson with what could be a problem class, and he hasn't bothered to sit in or even quiz me about my intentions.'*

"Right then, Mackay." I shouted as I threw the ball towards him, "We won't bother tossing a coin to choose ends, we'll stay as we are, and I'll show you how confident I am, YOU can have kick off."

The trap was set.

I blew the whistle as Billy stood there with his foot on top of the ball. He didn't move for a while, just looked at the class, smiled and posed. Then, as he took a couple of dribbling paces forward, I thundered in.

I hit the ball, HARD - my body followed on and went straight through the ball and then through Billy's legs. His body flew into the air and then came down with a crash. Mackay yelled, "That's a foul, that's a foul, you dirty b*****d."

I just towered over him on the floor and held the whistle up. "See this whistle, Mackay? That means *I'm* referee. I'll tell you what a foul is!"

"One nil," I shouted as I put the ball into the net and then returned it to the centre circle.

Billy Mackay glared at me. This time his cockiness had vanished, I saw fear in his eyes. He refused to come up to the ball.

"What's wrong, Billy? You were full of it two minutes ago. Surely a great footballer like you isn't beaten by one tackle and one goal?"

The arrogance was now replaced by a surliness, as he said. "That was a foul, it wasn't a fair goal."

"OK then, if you think so, I won't allow the goal, *this time.* Your kick off."

Reluctantly, he took the ball – but he wasn't sure.

I blew the whistle. He tapped it and then as I closed in he blasted it against the side wall and then sprinted past me after it. I was too fast for him, within ten metres I was past him, turned with the ball and dribbled towards *his* goal. I could hear his gasping breath behind me getting closer and closer. I knew that any second now he was going to scythe my legs from under me. So, I stopped dead, and stood on the ball. He splattered into my back and as I felt the contact I dug him in the ribs with my elbow, and once again he was rolling on the floor calling me a b*****d.

I ignored him this time, and shouted "Two-Nil."

Billy Mac, picked himself up, and sullenly slouched off the pitch to sit on the benches.

"That's two-nil Billy," I taunted him, "Surely the great sports star, who couldn't learn anything from a student, isn't finished already?"

Billy Mackay said nothing he just stared at his shoes.

"I'll tell you what Billy, we'll call that half time. I'll take kick off this time, and you can tackle me."

Mackay looked up, the evil smile on his face showed that he fancied his chance of revenge.

I kicked off, took two steps forward then stood on the ball. Billy sprinted in and crashed his right instep hard into my right shin. My lower leg felt like it was exploding, just like the cartoon victim often does on Tom & Jerry.

"Is that the best you can do?" I sneered at him.

So he obliged by kicking me twice more.

I showed no emotion even though the leg was now about to burst, I simply recommenced my dribble towards goal, aggressively brushed Billy aside, and shouted "Three-Nil," as I glared at the facetious pupil. I bellowed, "I think that proves my point, lads. Now go sit on that bench, Mackay, unless you want more?"

"Oh, and disturb me again, and next time you'll REALLY regret it."

We got on with the planned lesson, but Billy Mackay didn't join in.

I wasn't bothered.

Far too many teachers allow one misbehaving pupil to spoil the lesson for everybody. . . I wasn't about to allow that to happen. As lecturer Tony Milburn always stressed to us. "You can't teach a class *until* you have them under control."

As the class were filing out into the changing rooms, one of the lads stopped me and said, "Sir, that was the best lesson we've had for ages. They always get spoiled by BillyMac."

"Thanks son," I said, very pleased that I'd won over at least one fan.

I had one more, not particularly memorable, lesson before break, and then in the staffroom I discovered I had more than the one fan.

"Here, let me make this for you" an older member of staff said. "Have you got a mug?"

"I didn't think to bring one in."

"Never mind, I think this one is a spare."

I could see why nobody would use that one, it was chipped and really heavily stained, but as they say, 'don't look a gift horse in the mouth,' so I just said, "Thanks; coffee, two sugars."

"I hear you sorted out Billy Mackay for us. We've had problems with him for ages. He's been suspended at least four times, but he just comes back after his 'holiday' as bad as ever. We want to expel him but the Education Authority won't let us."

Then I felt a slap on my back, as another member of staff said, "Well Done, son. I hear you sorted Billy Mackay out for us."

Bloody Hell, I thought to myself, the word gets around this school pretty fast!

I didn't find out until my Teaching Practice was over that the reason Dewi Thomas hadn't come into that lesson, or indeed any future ones, was that the crafty Welshman had watched the whole incident from his room. All the time that I thought he was writing reports, he was sitting in front of the heating cupboard with the double doors open, watching every move I made through the grille. Then while I was covering his next lesson he was recounting the incident to other teachers in the staffroom.

As far as they were all concerned, I'd just passed my TP after only two days.

As far as I was concerned, I just wondered why nobody else had sorted him out before me. Dewi, also answered this puzzle when I left. "They all have mortgages, and wives and families to feed. They can't afford to lose their jobs. You have no responsibilities. It doesn't matter to you!"

I just nodded, but secretly thought to myself, *'I don't care how long I'd been in teaching, I would still react the same. I couldn't come into school everyday knowing that some kids were going to make my life hell. Maybe that's why I was considered a disciplinarian and they weren't. Maybe, also, that is why there are more teachers in mental hospitals, than any other profession!*

The staff, of Blandford Secondary might have given me the green light to pass my TP, but I still had to convince Mrs Baxter. She more or less kept out of my way for the first two weeks, apart from enquiring how I was settling in, obviously asking Dewi too, and checking on my lesson plans and crits.

I didn't have any problems from her until the fourth week when she tackled me on what I thought was a minor point. I had just come in from taking a rugby lesson on a drizzly day. I took off my boots, replaced them with my trainers, and entered the gym, to take a gymnastics lesson,

I thought it went quite well; so did she, except she pointed out that she wasn't impressed with the mud splashes that were up my tracksuit.

"I'd just come in from a rugby lesson," I retorted , irately, at her pettiness.

"Well, you should have, brought some clean kit with you, to change into!"

"I'm a student," I pointed out, "I'm not rich like you, I have *two* tracksuits and the other one is in the wash after yesterday's rugby lesson."

She conceded, "I understand that, but it might have been better to wear a dirty tracksuit out to rugby and keep the clean one for indoors."

"Then, one of them would never get washed, I have rugby every day."

"You have weekends to wash them."

"I play for the College team on Saturday's and the seven –a-side team on Sundays. I need a clean tracksuit for both."

"Well, if you can't sort something out, your dress will be reflected in your grade!"

Now she'd got me annoyed. "Look," I snapped, "If I was in danger of failing this Teaching Practice, I should have received a warning letter from you already!"

"I didn't say that you were in danger of failing, I'm just pointing out that it is possible to pass with a Distinction, a Credit or a simple Pass. Things like this make all the difference."

She wasn't happy when I said. "Well since I can't be failed at this stage – a rock bottom pass will suit me fine, thanks." Then I went over to the door and opened it for her to exit– I hoped that this show of politeness would gain me extra points!!!

*   *   *

Needless to say, I passed my final teaching practice without problem. That's not to say that I didn't have further problems in the School, however. . .

It was a beautiful sunny day when I was sitting in the staffroom having a coffee, and catching up on my lesson plans. The Headmaster entered, looked around and came straight over to me, "Oh, I'm glad I've found you, James. Mr Clarke, one of our English teachers has had to go home sick. Would you mind taking his class for him?"

"No problem," I said showing mock enthusiasm. "Whereabouts is it?"

"It's in the upper block, room 27, on the first floor. There's work set."

So, I set off for room 27. It was across the small quadrangle that separated the lower school from the upper. As it was so warm, all of the classrooms had their windows open. I could hear a riot going on from one of the classrooms.

I bet that's my class, I thought, as I neared the upper school.

The noise grew louder as I climbed the stairs to my cover lesson.

I opened the door to witness one of the pupils jumping from one desktop to another whilst the rest of the class tried to hit him with their books.

"**Mackay!**" I screamed."Sit down, or you won't be able to sit for the rest of this lesson!"

"Oh, f*****g hell, not you," he yelled back as ran across several more desktops, and jumped through the open window.

I quickly ran over to the window, visualising the headlines in the next day's newspaper. *"Pupil Throws Himself To His Death Whilst Trying To Get Away From Psycho Student Teacher!"*

I looked down expecting to see a tangled mess of bones and blood, - but, instead, saw a tiny dot of a figure running home across the fields whilst sticking up two fingers in the general direction of my window.

Once again, I was the hero of the staffroom, especially since Billy Mackay didn't just stay out of my lessons, but this time stayed away from school completely, until I'd left.

BillyMac, wasn't the only problem kid in the school, unfortunately, but he was the only problem that I experienced in PE.

However, PE wasn't the only subject I had to teach, I also had 4 periods a week of my second subject, Art, while I was at Blandford.

The first time I took 5b for a lesson, I was warned by the Head of Art, that they could be mischievous. Most of them were just filling in time until they left in the summer. They'd had lots of students, in the past, so maybe I could stop them from being bored by doing something a bit different.

That suited me fine, as I would rather do ceramics with them, so I was delighted when he agreed to my suggestion.

My first lesson with 5b was last period on Thursday, and I thought it went quite well. I showed them how to make thumb pots & coil pots, and then left them to experiment. At the end of the lesson they had to clean their benches, and the easiest way to remove clay is to first scrape off the excess, and then wash it down. So, I issued each bench with a fettling knife and a sponge.

With four minutes to the bell, all was shipshape - until I checked the equipment. Then I challenged the class, "Twelve knives were given out and have not been returned. Nobody will be leaving this room, when the bell goes, until they are handed in"

"Aw, sir, they're there, you haven't looked properly"

I glared at them, as I picked up, a piece of errant clay that hadn't made the recycle bin, I said, "Well, if you've put them in the wrong place, that mistake needs correcting. Nobody leaves until they are put HERE."

With the clay in my hand I opened the bin lid, and fortunately for a second took my attention off the class. As I looked in I saw twelve knives pointing at me blade up. If I'd put my hand in without looking . . . !!!

"Oh, that's very funny! But I don't appreciate the joke!

As you can't conduct yourselves properly, I will *not* be showing you how to throw a pot on the wheel next week. We'll go back to painting."

A collective, "Aw Sir, it was only a joke," was heard.

"Well, I don't think your jokes are funny. Off you go now, I look forward to seeing you next week," I said, tongue in cheek, desperate to let them see that they hadn't rattled me.

Before, the next Art lesson with 5b came around, I took the whole of that year, with Dewi, for Fifth Year games. I asked the Head of PE if it was alright that I joined in the rugby game, as I had missed my training sessions due to being on TP. He was OK with that, and suggested I played in the opposition team against the School team. As they were short of a hooker, I played out of position in the front row. I thought I had a good game: scrummaged well, often came out with the ball from mauls, went on a few good runs, etc.

As we were walking off the pitch, Wayne Burton, one of the 5b troublemakers, came up to me, "Thought you had a good game, there, Sir. Do you play for a team?"

"Only for the College team, now, but I used to play for Reading"

"Reading!!! They're one of the big teams round here – did you play for the first team?"

"Yeah, but it was two years ago when I played. Mind you we did win the County Cup that season.

I hope to play for them again next year, when I've finished College."

"I thought, from the way you played today, that you must have played for a big team!" Then, Burton ran off to tell the latest news to his mates.

Later in the week, when I took 5b for Art again, Burton was sitting on the back benches, as all troublemakers do, with his second row partner from the School team, Peter Jones.

I addressed the class, "Well, ladies and gentlemen, I told you last week that we were due to have had another pottery lesson today, but due to the stupid behaviour of some of you, we will go back to the basics in art. If you can prove yourselves worthy of it in the next couple of lessons we might progress onto to the potters' wheel, - but today, it will be Primary Colours."

I picked up a piece of chalk, "Not counting Black and White which technically aren't Primary Colours, there are . . ."

Just as I turned to the blackboard somebody made a stupid noise from the class, I quickly spun around to see Wayne Burton thump Peter Jones in the face, "*I've already warned you* - he's OK. *No* farting about!"

Pretending not to have seen or heard anything, I turned back to the board,

"There are three Primary Colours. Can anyone tell me what they are?"

One of the well behaved girls in the middle row put her hand up and said, "Red, yellow and blue, Sir."

"Thank you. Red – yellow – blue." Although I was talking to her, my eyes were using their peripheral vision to check on my rugby team chums. I was pretty certain I could see a red swelling developing around Jones' eye.

"Thank you, Jasmine. Yes, that is correct. . ."

The lesson continued successfully, and uninterrupted.

In fact, now that I had my enforcer sitting on the back row, I didn't have another problem for the full duration of my TP.

Although it was a rough school, I really enjoyed my stint at Blandford Secondary.

I gained a Credit for my efforts (which had been marked down from a Distinction due to my wardrobe problems).

At the end of my last lesson, Dewi came into the Sportshall and, embarrassingly, wished me goodbye in front of all the kids. Then as we walked out, he said to me, "You did well, there James, this is not an easy school to work in, you won over some new friends in the kids, but I don't think your supervisor was one of them."

I told him the story of my conflict over National Dance, and he nodded his head in approval, "Oh, that explains it. Well,

- well done to overcome both obstacles here."

I thanked him, and said, "I gained a Credit for this TP, so you obviously marked me high, as Mrs Baxter was sure to have downgraded me. How did you manage to do that since you never came into any of my lessons?"

Then Dewi, showed me his trick with the heating cupboard, and confessed that he also watched my every move outside, with the aid of binoculars, from the staffroom. He said he didn't need to hear or read my lesson content, as my tutor would do that, but he knew that if I could control and interest these classes then I would make a successful teacher.

I shook his hand, this time more vigourously, due to my new found respect for him.

*   *   *

Back at College, the pressure continued to mount as we approached our Finals.

I was really sticking in. I wasn't going to the bar until after 9 pm every night, and then went back to my room, after time was called (no parties), drank moderately, and was even sober enough, most nights (weekends not included) to write up notes, etc.

So when my sociology lecturer, Dave Zephyr, (I think he was Polish), called into the SU for a pint one evening I was well prepared.

"You know, Jimbo, it is a real pleasure to have you in my tutorial group. Our discussions are always lively with you there. You always make an interesting contribution, but that's not going be enough to get you through the Finals, OR get the pass grade that you need. You are going to have to start producing essays on time, and stick in to your revision."

"Dave," I said, "don't worry, I've got it all sorted." Then I turned to the barman, "Alf, get this fine fellow another Guinness."

"Well, I admire your confidence; but, confidence isn't going to get you the pass you need."

"Dave, you're a worrier, Chill. I'll do it." I said, "Cheers," as I chinked his glass.

He wished me well, as I left him at the bar to rejoin the rugby lads in the corner.

He needn't have worried.

I passed all my Final exams with flying colours. (Well - not quite flying! In most I just scraped through – but, as you already know, 'scraping' was enough for me). However, at Sociology, I excelled and achieved the third highest score in my group.

"Well, Jimbo, I don't know how you did it," Dave Z told me as he ordered a celebration pint for me at the S.U. bar, "but I've got to admire your confidence."

"Dave, as a sociology lecturer, you should know – most sociology is just waffle! I spent the last three weeks just reading up and learning the key words. Then after I'd memorised all these buzz words I just built a bullshit essay around these words in the exam."

"Well, you said you'd do it, so well done," he replied, as he raised his glass. "It's not a method that I'm going to recommend to future students, but it worked for you. Well Done!"

In fact, it worked in every subject, even the History of Education – which I hated. What I didn't tell Dave, however, was that for the last month before the Finals I cranked up the gears. I limited myself to two or three pints a night (except weekends), and worked every night (except weekends!!!)

until two or three in the morning – and still made breakfast and 9 am lectures! I was a reformed man – but could only keep it up for a month!!!

I don't think even Dave Zephyr would have believed it if I had told him that in the future I would take 'O' level Sociology classes for nearly a year at one of my Supply Teaching schools.

*　　　　*　　　　*

Outside of Exams and Teaching Practice there was still plenty of time to relax. Of course this mainly revolved around weekends and rugby.

I was selected to play fly half for the South West Colleges Team which played against the South East Colleges in the Southern Trial at Cheltenham.

I had a good game, and gave my opposite number the run around, even though I was on the beaten team. So obviously I was amazed when he still gained selection over me!?

However they were kind enough to select me as first reserve for the backs. So, I was delighted when one of our players dropped out and I was promoted to play in the Final England Colleges Trial playing for the South against my birthplace of the North. Unfortunately, I wasn't so keen at being picked out of position – especially as I was on the wing, marking British Lions representative Peter Squires!!!

The first time I got the ball – in acres of space – I went head to head with Squires. I jinked to the left; he moved to cover. I jinked to the right; he moved across again. Then left, then right, then left again. I had him fooled, he had no idea where I was going – (that was understandable, 'cos I had no idea where I was going either.) He moved in to tackle me and as I was almost in his grasp, I made one last jink to the right and I was free. Running as fast as my legs could take me. A big smile on my face as I had just put a British Lions player on his backside.

I didn't have time to smile for long, though, because although I have described many times before I was like a whippet – Peter Squires was like a rocket. Within 25 metres he had regained his feet again, sprinted after me and flattened me before I made the line.

I suffered his explosive speed three more times during the game as he ran in a hat-trick of tries.

Needless to say; I wasn't selected for The English Colleges team that took on the Welsh Colleges later that month.

I had just been taught a lesson as to how good you needed to be to play at international level, and just to put another nail into the coffin of my international aspirations, soon afterwards my College team played a friendly against London Welsh.

It was only a 'friendly' Sunday fixture against London Welsh Newts (their social 'drinking' team) but they still had several current and ex-internationals in the line up. One of whom was the current British Lions Number Eight, Derek Quinnell.

Quinnell was playing tactically in immediate conflict with me - one of his favourite moves was to pick up the ball at the back of the scrum and head directly for the opposing fly half, not only to batter him, but also to tie him up in the resultant maul, giving his backs a one man advantage.

The first time he tried it, I was ready for him, as he ran towards me I drove in low, crashed my left shoulder into his thigh in one of the most aggressive tackles that I'd ever made. I reached my arms out to encompass his legs, and . . . to my horror, my little arms (I was only five foot seven) weren't long enough to stretch around the enormous thigh muscles of his six foot seven frame.

I did all that I could and grabbed firmly onto just one of his legs. That didn't bring him down, but slowed him until reinforcements ran in to stop him. The incident didn't last long, but to me seemed like an eternity as Quinnell ran on for a further twenty metres, constantly trying to swat me off with his spare hand, like an annoying little fly. I felt like one of those cowboys who, in the film, had been knocked off his horse and dragged along with his foot still trapped in the stirrup!

My confidence was at an all time low, after my two skirmishes with these two 'Lions' players, but was partly restored when I played against the current England fly half in the British Colleges Sevens at Wasps ground. I tackled him out of the game, and made several good breaks which set us up for a good win over his College. After the game the Wasp's Secretary asked me who I was playing for the following season, after I had left College. I replied that it really depended where I could get a job. He asked me if I would play for his Club if I gained employment close enough. I was delighted and agreed, but unfortunately all of my local interviews failed to bear fruit and I ended up going home to play for Middlesbrough, later Stockton, and finally Acklam.

Hard work and long hours at my Schools meant that I didn't have as much time, energy or enthusiasm to apply to my personal rugby – putting paid to my blossoming rugby ambitions!

Back at College, the rugby season was finally drawing to a close. There was only one last major fixture to satisfy – The Annual Rugby Club Dinner. It was to be held at The Pheasant Pluckers Bar & Restaurant in Henley - on - Thames. The guest speaker was to be Mr. Bill Stevens.

Yes, Bill Stevens, Head of the PE Department – the very bloke who had set me up for my final teaching practice with the tutor who disliked me the most. Time for revenge!

We had all finished a superb meal, and several drinks, when a glass was chinkled and Big Bill stood up to speak. Then the catcalls started, "Stand up, stand up . . . etc!

He raised his hands to appeal for silence.

"Ladies and gentlemen, I would like to thank you for this great honour . . ."

That was when the first bread roll went whistling past his ear. *Blast! Bad shot*, I thought, but the next one hit him smack in the chest. Then everybody, (unplanned), joined in and the big bun fight had started. Big Bill hid under the table. The manager came in with reinforcements and threw us out telling us never to go there again.

I felt partially vindicated.

Before the end of term, more reprisals were to come from other students, but I'd like to put the record straight right now:- it wasn't me that put John Busker's motorbike up on the roof of Mitford Hostel. The staff couldn't prove it was me, but I couldn't provide an alibi, either so that suspicion still hung over me. However, only I knew it couldn't be me, as the last time anybody saw me that night was in Chequers, in Woodley village. When I went to the toilet, a bit worse for wear, at the end of the night, the rest of my buddies set off walking the half mile back to College, without me. Somehow, I didn't make it all the way back, and fell asleep on a bench at the side of our cricket pitch. Only a few squirrels and foxes were there to bear witness.

I'm surprised Tony Milburn didn't grill them too!!!

*   *   *

After the rugby season and then the Finals had finished, College almost petered out. Lectures were no more and third year students were left with an abundance of time to apply for jobs and attend interviews.

I attended numerous interviews all around the London area, but was offered none. Sometimes I was pleased, after attending the interview, that I wasn't offered anything (maybe that came across in the interview) but at others I was hopeful.

I was also applying to several companies for a holiday job to help pay off my overdraft (more of that in the next chapter), but everything was knocked out of synch when very late and low on my list of applications Cleveland Education Committee offered me a job. They were so desperate for a teacher at Harry Mac's, that they asked me to start immediately.

I said a tearful farewell to my buddies in the PE department (and outside of it), and called in at Big Bill's house to thank him for putting up with me and also to make peace after our recent conflicts.

He said, "Jimbo, I'll never forget you - you were like a bloody rubber ball, every time we knocked you down, you came bouncing back again. But, I enjoyed working with you," he shook my hand, and continued, "you'll make a good teacher. Good Luck."

So there I was, lost.

I felt abandoned.

A major part of my life had just ended, I had passed all of my exams and Teaching Practices, and now I was thrown out into the real world. I'd only gone to College to enjoy myself and experience three years of playing rugby – and other sports, but now it had all finished. I felt totally empty.

Of course, I could opt out of teaching, take any other job that I was offered and stay down South, playing for Wasps or Reading, but that would disappoint my Mother greatly. Besides I wouldn't be FULLY qualified until I'd completed my 'Probationary' year. So I accepted the offer of a job in Cleveland, determined to do just the one year and then to return South for rugby.

The rest is history – and all recounted in the book – "FATED . . . but I never wanted to be a teacher."

Chapter 9

Holiday Jobs

As has been frequently mentioned in previous chapters, a lot of my holiday time from College was taken up by trying to pay off my ever growing bank overdraft by working in various holiday jobs.

I have devoted an entire chapter to this subject because, not only have I some funny stories to tell, but I believe these jobs were an integral part in my development both as a person, and as a teacher.

Too many people in education, when growing up, leave school – go on to university – and then go back to school to work as a teacher. They have no experience of anything else in life except their own subject and academic pursuits. I don't think this is beneficial to either the teacher, or the children.

I believe this drawback is well illustrated by a science teacher that I knew at one of the early schools that I taught in. He was a very likeable man, and much better qualified than the majority of teachers who merely have a Bachelor of Education degree. He was a Doctor (of Science) and could probably easily write out the complex formula for advanced rocket fuel, BUT the kids ran riot in his lessons. He needed to get SIMPLE science across to them. They just needed to pass a GCSE exam, or at most GCE 'A' level. He undoubtedly knew his subject inside out, and found it easy, but couldn't put it across to most of the kids that were struggling with the basics. Added to that he wasn't good on discipline, so the kids ran riot in his lessons and learnt very little.

I believe that every teacher needs to have a great deal of varied experiences before they face their first class, and that at interview they should be rejected if they haven't any other additions to their CV apart from academic.

My own spirit of adventure, my hitch-hiking, Duke of Edinburgh's Award experiences and holiday job escapades made me, I'm sure, into a much better, more rounded teacher, that understood kids far better because of this background.

That is why I place so much importance on this chapter.

I didn't actually start my first holiday job when I was at College, but two years before – my first year in the Sixth Form at Acklam Hall.

I was just seventeen, and hadn't even had a paper round, before I started working for the local refuse department as a binman. I knew that the 'gang' that I was allocated to weren't keen to have 'another bloody student' working with them, so I had it tough right from the start. However, as soon as I started f*ing & blinding the same as they did from day one, *and* could also shift the pints after our days work *and* could graft as hard as them during the shift, I was accepted, and became one of the boys.

As I was only seventeen I was too young to be allowed to lift the heavy bins onto the cart (no wheelie bins in those days) but after week three I insisted on doing this, because even though I was the smallest in the 'gang' I was certainly the strongest. After week four, I think they regretted this promotion. They thought I was a slave driver as I rushed them along so that we could finish earlier on each Friday, in order to make the pub by dinnertime. In the boozer, my status increased even further, and I earned my nickname of 'Prof' because I was clever enough to finish Sam Spudikins (Salvation Army) crossword in record time, which most of them *really* struggled with.

The gang accepted me so much that they now took to playing practical jokes on me. I often saw through these pranks, but went along with them anyway.

The most common of these was one of the gang wanting to change sides of the street that we were working, "because he was bored with that side!"

That clearly meant that there was a vicious dog coming up, or a bolshy customer.

There were times that they did catch me by surprise, however. Like the time they all stood around laughing while I struggled to lift the bin outside of a local shop that was always full of broken glass and weighed a ton. They thought it was hilarious as I almost gave myself a hernia trying to lift the bin, which eventually took three of us to put into the wagon.

They also thought it was incredibly funny after they had lined me up to lift the broken bin at a local Chinese Restaurant. It was always full of stinking meat – that I believed to be chicken. When I lifted it to my shoulders to load onto the wagon, the bottom fell out and I was covered in mouldy meat, and hundreds of accompanying maggots. They gang fell about in hysterics, as I frantically struggled to get out of my overalls and was flailing with both hands to rid myself of the pests. For some reason they thought it was even more hilarious when I berated them, whilst standing in just my underpants in the middle of a busy shopping precinct.

The last holiday job that I worked at before going to College was at a laundry in Hull. I had written all over the place to Teesside companies for work, but eventually had to take my reserve option of working for my uncle in the laundry that he managed, *and living with him, and my Aunty, for six weeks.*

That was the hardest part because my Aunt still thought of me as the little boy that she used to take to Middlesbrough football matches, when I had just started grammar school. As I was 18 now, she found it difficult to accept my coming in after midnight most nights, especially after I had had one or two shandies to drink!!!

Some of other workers in the factory also found it difficult to accept me, as they were suspicious that I was the boss's 'spy'. I think the day that we had a stand up row and I was f*ing & blinding at him for accusing me of doing something that I hadn't, convinced them that I wasn't his puppet.

Once I had become one of the lads, I started dating 'one of the girls.' Which could have been nice, except that it almost landed me in hospital.

After I had been seeing Kathryn for a couple of weeks, she suggested we go out in a foursome with her best friend, Jenny, and boyfriend Paul. I agreed, but if I'd known Paul's background in advance, maybe I wouldn't. He'd been in trouble with the Police on several occasions, mainly for GBH, and was well known as a hot head.

So I might have reconsidered stepping in when during an argument on the way home from the pub, he started punching and kicking his girlfriend. Stupidly, I went over and said, "Come on you two, we've had a good night, there's no need to spoil it like this."

Without warning, Paul yelled, "Who the f*****g hell asked you?" and jumped on me putting me in a headlock. I was so surprised, I hadn't expected this response, and before I could react he tried to push my face down onto a spiked metal fence. I quickly snapped my head to the side as one of the spikes just missed my left eye and luckily only made a moderate cut down the side of my face, just above the cheek bone. Fortunately it didn't need stitches. As I recovered my composure, I quickly put my left arm across the top of the railings so that now he was merely bouncing my head up and down on my own forearm. I tried, in vain, to wriggle my head out of his grip, but years of manual work had built up the muscles in his arms to develop a vice like grip. So, as Paul tried a second, third and fourth time to put my eyes out on this fence I changed my tactics and started punching him in the back, trying to fell him with a kidney punch. Now, under normal circumstances, just one, or at the most two of these, would have floored a normal person, but this lad was not normal, he was a maniac. It took four punches to stop him. Then, as I swore at him, we parted company, and I didn't see him for another week.

Jenny came into work the next day and apologised for what had happened and said that Paul was off sick, I'd really hurt him, and he was going to the doctor's later that day.

Paul came back to work the following week, but I didn't get an apology from him. We just avoided each other. I was thankful that this was my last week before going off to College, otherwise another confrontation seemed inevitable.

In October I started Bulmershe College, and it seemed only a matter of days before we were on holiday again, this time for Christmas.

Before going away to College, another of my aunties had fixed me up with a holiday job as a barman at the Grand Hotel in Middlesbrough. What an eye opener that was!!!

The Grand, has now been closed down for many years, but when it was in its heyday, it was famous throughout the North and by seamen throughout the world!

It was just opposite the railway station and less than a mile from the docks. It was very common for foreign sailors, who spoke very little English, to have been recommended by other countrymen or sailors, to head for the Grand if they wanted a good night.

The Grand it may have been called – but grand it certainly wasn't when I worked there. When it was first built and newly decorated - maybe; but when I worked there in the winter of 1969 it was a bit beyond its best. There were two bars downstairs and an upstairs dance hall. The bars downstairs were 'Grandly' named the Palm Lounge (where many of the 'Ladies' hung out) and the Diamond Bar which was the domain of the gay fraternity (male and female).

An innocent young 19 year old certainly had his eyes opened here! There was much wheeling and dealing between the girls, and the foreign sailors, and generally the Ladies took the seamen for a ride (in more ways than one) – but there was also a code of honour which many of the 'girls' adhered to.

It was very common for me to witness a girl invite a sailor back to her place after he had been buying her drinks all night. The poor sailor was so drunk that he didn't know what he was doing, so once he agreed, his date would ask if they should take some more drink back with them and maybe some fags too?

The positive response from the matelot meant that they were paying bar prices for a bottle of vodka, Bacardi, or the like, and always at least 100 cigarettes. The poor foreigner, not understanding the currency always just offered up a handful of banknotes, and I took what was due. Then he staggered out of the bar with his arm around his female friend, who I am sure looked absolutely gorgeous through his beer goggles.

On one particular night, I witnessed these goings on for the umpteenth time, when unfortunately the particular sailor concerned, crashed out before he could make it back to 'her place.' As he collapsed unconscious to the bar floor, his wallet, stuffed with ten pound notes, fell out of his hand, and spilled open. A crowd gathered around it, ready to pounce, when his 'date' stood up, astride his unconscious body and said. "Anyone touch that wallet, and I'll have their f***ing eyes out with this bottle."

It seemed that Pauline, one of our regulars, didn't mind robbing him blind when he was still sober enough to consent, but wouldn't take advantage of him once he had blacked out.

"Here, Jimbo," she said to me as she handed over the wallet. "He'll probably come back for that tomorrow."

That's why I always had a soft spot for Pauline.

All the locals nicknamed her 'Big Spender', and for good reason. When she was having a good week and plenty of money in her purse, she would buy everyone a drink.

"How's it going, Pauline?" I would ask, as she came in.

"Great, Jim. If I had another pair of legs, I would open up in Newcastle!"

"What'll it be then?"

"A Bloody Mary for me, and a drink for all of my friends," she would say with a grand sweep of her hand to gesture around the bar. Everybody would crowd in for their treat.

But, I also saw Pauline on her barren days when she was depressed and was wondering where the money was going to come from to pay for the electricity in her house. She would slump onto her bar stool, and I could tell before I asked. "How's it going, Pauline?"

"Terrible, Jimmy. I've walked me fr*****g legs off. I've just got to get the fr*****g weight off these." And just after her bum hit the bar stool she would slump her ample breasts onto the bar, to ease the strain.

"What'll it be then?"

"Just a tomato juice, Jim."

Funny, at that point, not one of her friends crowded the bar to pay back the numerous drinks she'd bought them.

As I poured her tomato juice, I would always slip a vodka into it, to make it (near enough) into her usual Bloody Mary. She would always respond with, "Thanks

Jim, I'll see you're alright when the tide turns.

Throughout the night, as one or two of the older regulars came in, Big Spender had a few more drinks bought by her real friends, buy she never recouped the money she gave out.

I was quite sad when I heard that Pauline had died several years ago, she didn't have much of a life, but she loved her kids and her true friends.

*   *   *

For my next two summers my holiday jobs were both with British Steel, with another Christmas stint at The Grand jammed in between them.

The two stints working in the Steelworks couldn't have been more different: the first was with a sub-contractor, cleaning out blast furnaces and rolling mills, and the second working in the Company's own chemical laboratories.

The first was at the Hartlepool Steelworks and was only for two weeks when the whole of the plant shut down for its annual holiday. I earned more money working twelve hour shifts for fourteen days without break in this job than I did in the eight weeks I worked in the laundry – but it was arduous. It would have been much, much harder, if I hadn't been put in a gang with "Jack the Lad."

On the very first day when our 'gang' of total strangers was put together, 'Jack' took control. It was our job to clean out all of the fallen 'clinkers' which were overflowing from under one of the Rolling Mills. The access to this area was down some steps and then through an inspection hatch, which took us to the underside of the huge stainless steel rollers.

It was so full there that even to be able to take one step inside the hatch we had to work for two hours to shift tons of clinkers *(iron scraps that fell of the hot metal as it was being rolled along)*.

"Hey, what are you doing?" Jack asked as he watched me work (Jack was good at this – he often watched people work).

"Doing what you said," I replied quizzically.

"Well you're doing it all wrong."

"All you said was shovel those clinkers up to the top of the steps from the hatch and you'd shovel them into the skip, to be taken away. I didn't know there was a wrong or a right way to shovel!"

"There's nowt wrong with your shovelling," he said, "it's just that you're doing it too fast! If we all work at this rate, the job will be finished before the end of this week, and they'll only move us on to another one. Slow down!!!"

Jack had it all worked out, three of us worked - slowly – at the inspection hatch to clear a space and three were up on top shovelling the waste into a skip that was taken away by the foreman for disposal.

Once we had cleared sufficient space for all three of us to get inside the inspection hatch, Jack disappeared.

He came back a few minutes later with three big cardboard boxes. He flattened them and then called us all to his 'union' meeting inside the hatch as we all sat on them.

"This is how we work it from now on boys. Now we've cleared a space, this is our rest area. We go in 3 gangs of two – choose your partner. Then only four work while two rest. We'll draw lots for who rests first after we've all built up a stock in the first three hours."

Alan, who was as green as me (and became my work partner) asked, "What if the bosses find out that we're not all working?"

"They won't," Jack retorted, as long as they see clinkers coming out of the hatch they'll think we're all working. Besides, they're not going to crawl under the mills and get their clean suits or overalls dirty. Anyway I'll be up top to explain what's happening."

That's right Jack – you get the cushy job.

It all worked exactly as Jack had planned it. For the first three hours four of us worked hard under the mill, stockpiling the clinkers at the entrance. One bloke shovelled them slowly from the entrance up to Jack, who even more slowly threw them into a skip. After 3 hours, pair A took a spell off in our cardboard lined restroom, while B and C worked. After another 3 hours pair B rested while A & C worked and so on. Al and myself were pair A which meant we rested first. I wasn't keen on this, but as we all drew lots fairly, I had to just grin and bear it. I would have much preferred to have worked nine hours and have the last three off.

When this system was first suggested by Jack, I felt a bit guilty not working the full twelve hour shift that we were being paid for, but later, on reflection, I realised that none of us would have made the full fourteen days of the contract if we had worked twelve hours at the speed we set off at. On completion of our stint, our gang delivered up a spotlessly clean rolling mill which had been our given mission.

For two weeks all I had done was work, sleep, work. I'd had no social life but made stacks of money. I was totally knackered, it was by far the most strenuous job I'd ever had.

In total contrast, the next time I worked for British Steel, I was employed in the easiest job that I'd ever had. It was in the Labs. at the Cleveland Works in South Bank. I was given the job because I wrote on the application form that I had passed 'O' level Chemistry and when I was interviewed (over the phone) I knew how to do a 'titration'. The 'Lab's' only directive was to analyse samples of iron ore, when they came into Teesport on the big ocean going cargo ships, We had to evaluate how pure the ore was, and once the figures were known, the bosses from both Companies would haggle over the price for the shipment. If we were happy with the price, the ship would be unloaded and that ore used to produce iron and steel in Cleveland. If an agreement on price could not be met, the captain would keep his cargo and set off down the coast to try to sell it at Scunthorpe, or beyond.

So it was vital that British Steel had these iron ore samples analysed and results produced *quickly and accurately.*

Ninety per cent of the time we did this within half an hour, but if our negotiators weren't happy with the figures, then the samples would be sent back to be re-analysed. Although this sounds complicated and difficult – it was quite easy! It was like baking a cake. My job was to determine how much Sulphur was in my sample. So I sloshed a few ingredients together in a flask and then poured in some acid, and as I added the acid I measured how much it took to turn the blue liquid clear – *Done!* – that was the number they wanted. It took about twenty minutes. – and this is why I claimed it was my easiest job – we only received at most, two, ore carrying, ships a day into Teesport. On a really busy day, if re-tests had to be done, we would work about one hour and twenty minutes! But I was paid three times more than I would be as a teacher. No wonder British Steel failed to compete successfully on the World Stage!

I worked in these labs for eight weeks, and got on really well with my colleagues. So much so, that in our regular morning discussions where we discussed the morning news and world events, they all ganged up on me and tried to persuade me to stay on in the job permanently. The supervisor told me, "Before you came we'd been advertising for an extra chemist for months. I'm certain if you want it, the job's yours."

"Hey, thanks for the tip, but I'd rather become a teacher."

"But, you've already told us how poor the wage is and about the excessive workload. Why would anybody want to give up a cushy, well paid job like this, to live on a pauper's wage?"

"I've told you fellas before why! This job is good money but it's boring. Twenty minutes work a day??? I've read more books and newspapers since I've been here than I have in the whole of my life. I'm a Grand Master at sudoku and crosswords now. Teaching might be poorly paid, but it's interesting, and we work so hard that we don't have time to be bored!"

"So that's final then," Dave the second in command said, "It doesn't matter what we say, you're gonna condemn yourself to a pauper's life regardless."

I nodded, and said, "I think you're being a bit dramatic with all this pauper business. The wage isn't great, but it's hardly breadline!"

"Well, OK," the boss said, in that case we've all chipped in to buy you a leaving present."

He handed over a cylindrical, beautifully wrapped package with "I hope that you put it to good use."

As I tore the wrapping paper open, the four of them roared with laughter as I held up my very own glass beaker.

The joke was, that when I arrived there for my first day at work, when the tea trolley came around at 10.30 am I produced my very own sparklingly new mug, but the rest of them simply threw out the chemicals from a previous titration, swilled the beaker out once with cold water, and presented it to the tea lady for replenishment.

I never did get into their system, thus the engraving on the side of the beaker which read "We hope you enjoy many, many coffees out of this, specially designed, drinking vessel."

When I left I presented the boss with my coffee mug (only one careful owner!).

In between these stints with British Steel (as I've already mentioned) I spent my last Christmas Break as a barman in the Grand. This wasn't particularly significant in that I had already seen the sights, but in this stint I also saw the more violent side of life in the gutter.

As well as the prostitutes that frequented our hostelry were, I'm sure, their pimps and other members of the local underworld. So violence was never very far from surfacing.

One example of this, was the night when one of the older 'girls came running into the bar. Scotch Lizzie, ran up to Pauline and asked, "Has Jimmy been in?"

When Pauline shook her head, she added, loudly, so that everybody in the bar heard, "Well if he does, you haven't seen me. I haven't been in!"

Jimmy, her husband, was a rather unsavoury character who had just been released from Durham Jail. He was looking for Lizzie because he had heard that while he'd been in jail, that she had been with another man – *(even though Lizzie was a prostitute and he was her pimp!!!)*

As it happened, Jimmy didn't come into the Grand that night – the Police did.

They asked everybody if they'd seen either Scotch Lizzie or Jimmy that night, and of course everybody shook their heads and had seen nothing.

Then, as he was leaving the lead copper said to the collective clientele, "Well if Jimmy comes in phone us." He had a look on his face that showed that he knew he was wasting his breath. "Lizzie's fighting for her life in hospital. She was stabbed several times in a phone box just outside the Town Hall."

Very little of the violent underbelly of the area was displayed inside the pub itself, in fact on reflection I would say that we probably had less trouble than most other pubs I'd been in. However, because of the character of some of the clientele, it was bound to happen sometimes. Very rarely, however, were the bar staff threatened, but on one particular weekend close to Christmas, it did happen.

The place was heaving. Customers were six deep at the bar, all yelling their orders at once. At my end of the bar, I was trying to memorise the order that customers had arrived in, so that they were served when it was their turn, just as one voice boomed over the others. "I'll have 4 pints of beer and 4 whisky chasers, barman."

I heard it clearly, but as there were at least seven people before him, I ignored it.

After I served that customer, I looked to find who I thought was the next customer, when the voice boomed out again, "Oi, are you deaf, I said I'll have 4 pints of beer and 4 whisky chasers."

This time I reacted, with a lot more courtesy than he'd shown, "Just one moment, sir, there are a couple of other customers first."

"F*** the other customers," he yelled as he pushed past people to get closer, "If I don't get served next I'm gonna ram this glass into your ugly face."

I finished the order I was on, and immediately rang upstairs for the manager.

Then I ignored bully boy, and served another customer.

"I'm warning you a******e, I'd better . . ."

The door swung open next to me and Stuart, the manager walked in.

"What's the problem?"

I turned my back on the bar, and said to the manager, "Can you see the fella over my right shoulder, dark navy suit, mauve shirt?"

There are about five people in front of him, to be served, but he's threatened to glass me if I don't serve him next."

"OK, I'll deal with this," he said, then he stepped up to the bar, and greeted the thug with a cheery smile and said, "Now then, Bernie, what seems to be the problem?"

"It's not me, it's that f*****g cheeky little b******d who refuses to serve me. I'm gonna do 'im with that attitude."

"Now, Bernie, there's no need for that. I'm going to look after you now. What is it you want?"

Stuart managed to pacify the abusive Bernie, and then turned to me and said, "He's drunk, he's normally OK. I've served him loads of times before, never had any trouble from him. Just in case though, I would order a taxi to take you home tonight."

After we had called time, and cajoled the last customer to go home, the staff sat down to have a relaxing drink together while I waited for my cab. Elsie, the barmaid who was working with me that night, said "Do you know who that was, that you had the argument with tonight? He was Bernie, one of John McLean's boys."

In my naivety I asked, "Who the f*** is John McLean?"

"John McLean?" Elsie gasped, "You don't know John McLean? He's only the biggest gangster in Cleveland, and Bernie's one of his boys!"

That night I waited inside the pub for the taxi driver to come in and collect me and escort me out. I examined every shadow for movement before I quickly crossed the five yards of pavement to open the taxi door. It was only when we turned the corner into Laycock Street, that I began to breathe easily.

I only had two more weeks to go, until I returned to College, and fortunately, neither Bernie or John Mc, set foot inside the Grand while I was there.

*   *   *

My final holiday job before starting life as a full time teacher was a bit of a funny one, because, due to the unusual circumstances.

I had already worked for four weeks as a teacher at Harry Mac's School in Stockton and I definitely needed a break.

However, as they say, a change is as good as a rest, so I became the Playscheme Co-ordinator at Beechwood Youth Club in Middlesbrough.

I didn't get much of a rest!!!

Beechwood Youth Club, by its name conjures up visions of an idyllic rustic old building, set in the centre of a beautiful copse full of beech trees swaying in a gentle warm summer breeze: - but nothing could be further from the truth – it was set in one of the most deprived areas of Middlesbrough, with, as far as I know, no forest there, and very few beech trees. The building was of an ugly modernistic design, yellow brick with a huge sloping roof that we were constantly telling the kids off for climbing up and down, as they accidently (or otherwise) broke the tiles, resulting in even more buckets catching the leaks when it rained.

The kids, who attended the Youth Club were little roughnecks, with very little discipline at home, so some took badly to discipline at their leisure centre.

Unfortunately for them, I laid down the law from day one, and 80% of the kids respected this. Of the other twenty percent, three quarters of them played up but settled down after a warning of being thrown out, or backed off when they saw me kick out the five per cent who just wouldn't heed my warnings. Most of the warnings were for trivial things like vandalism, swearing, playing five a side or basketball with outdoor shoes on, etc., but as I've stated before: if you pick up on the trivial bits of misbehaviour, then the big bits of misbehaviour hardly ever develop.

When being thrown out of the youth centre I was regularly provoked by the offender with, "I'm gonna tell my older brother about this, and he'll come down here and sort you out!"

"OK, son, can you tell your brother to be here early 'cos we finish here at four o'clock and I'll be on my way home by quarter past."

This calling of their bluff worked every time, but I was always still fearful of some man mountain calling at the centre asking for me!

The majority of the kids, however, were just playful, under-privileged urchins who were thankful for the activities that we arranged for them.

One thing that did surprise me, however, and prompted me into further action, was being told by a bunch of the kids one day that they had never been to the seaside.

The youth club was only ten miles from Redcar, our nearest resort, but these teenagers had never seen the sea!!!

On checking I found that the vast majority of kids on this playscheme had never been to Redcar!

So I promised them that if they helped me to raise the money, that in the last week I would organise a bus trip to Redcar.

We made it into Project Seaside, and formed a small committee of the kids who decided that the way we would raise the funds necessary would be to organise a jumble sale. The kids were great, they made their own leaflets advertising the event and asking for jumble donations. The four other playleaders involved themselves (and the kids) in baking cakes for a cakestall and organising the painting of posters to go up in local shops. The kids committee organised the rest of our playscheme into groups to deliver the leaflets and collect the jumble. I, in turn, co-erced my mother into selling on the jumble stall whilst I left myself free to deal with problems.

Imagine my horror then, when on the day, one of the problems I had to deal with was two young towrags who had stolen (off their own friends and fund) from the jumble stall.

My mother was almost in tears when she came to me and said "See those two lads there. They've stolen two vinyl records from my stall. The one in the anorak has them up his jumper."

As I approached the boys, they knew something was up because they increased their pace, but I cut them off before they reached the door. "What's that up your jumper?" I asked the lad in the anorak.

"Nothing," was his anticipated reply.

"Nothing?" I reiterated with an astonished expression. "I can see the shape of two records sticking out of your jumper. – ***Go and put them back!***"

"We've paid for them."

"Funny, a minute ago you didn't have anything up your jumper. Now you've just remembered that you've paid for them. Hand them over or I'm calling the police."

He shoved them into my hand and in a very hurt tone said, "I'm telling my brother about you!"

"Well while you're telling him that son, tell him that you are now both banned from the seaside trip that you tried to steal the money from."

The two culprits slouched out and we never saw them again.

The fundraiser was a great success, because of it we hired a 59 seater bus and took 48 teenagers plus 5 playleaders to a very windy but sunny Redcar. Each kid received a goody bag of a couple of sandwiches for lunch, an orange drink, a bar of chocolate and a small amount of spending money for ice creams or amusements. There was even a little left over with which we bought more sweets to give as prizes for the three legged race, egg & spoon, etc. that we organised on the beach. Everyone had a great time, and I was really pleased to give those deserving kids a day out that they'll never forget.

*   *   *

And that leads us nicely, to the first day of my teaching career at The Harold MacMillan Secondary School for Boys.
This of course is covered in depth in my first book, "FATED . . . but I never wanted to be a teacher."

If you would like to comment on either of these books, or, indeed, check on the progress of the last book in this Trilogy, "Calamity James," then log in to facebook and access the group "The James Masters Appreciation Society" which keeps members updated.

I would also appreciate any reviews that readers would like to submit to Amazon.

At the time of going to press "Fated" was rated at 4.8 stars, and generally assessed as 'very funny' – I hope that this book lives up to that high standard.

I'm sure you'll let me know!!!

Other Publications by the Author

<u>In Paperback</u>   "Working in Sport"
              How To Books . . .   3 editions
Ever fancied a job in Sport but didn't want to teach, join the Army, or work in a sports centre? This book contains information on how to get a variety of sports related jobs whatever your level of skill / qualifications.

<u>In Paperback & ebooks through Amazon</u>
"Fated . . . but I never wanted to be a teacher"
A hilarious comic autobiography about the trials and tribulations of a young teacher.

As a youngster, James Masters hadn't the slightest intention of going to university, and at eighteen had already taken out the forms to become a Physical Training Officer in the RAF.

Through a number mishaps and coincidences he did eventually qualify as a teacher, but still unsure that this really was the job for him, attempted to leave on three separate occasions:- each time being pulled back, as if on an elastic!

Fated . . . is an easy to read book, which won't win the Nobel Prize for literature, (so Shakespeare & Dickens can rest easy), but will keep you entertained to the end.

It is hard to believe that all of the disasters and mishaps happened to one person, but, truthfully, they did. James Masters seemed to be a disaster magnet!!! Incredibly, all of the stories *are* true.

It is rated on Amazon, by reviewers, at 4.8 out of 5 stars.

<u>Website</u>   Skiing on a Shoestring.com
Website of the day on Radio Two; it details how you can go Skiing or snowboarding (whether first time or experienced) much cheaper than you thought possible. Tips on tour operators, travel, accommodation and equipment, to fit in with the tightest of budgets.

<u>COMING SOON</u> - on Amazon ebooks
"Calamity James"
The sequel to his previous two books.
It tells the hilarious story of many of James' numerous misadventures outside of teaching, and after he had eventually retired.

Written in the same easy style as the two previous books, this one should have you laughing and entertained to the end too!!!

Printed in Great Britain
by Amazon